ROCK&ROLL ARCHAEOLOGIST

How I Chased Down Kurt's Stratocaster, the "Layla" Guitar, and Janis's Boa

PETER BLECHA

SASQUATCH BOOKS
SEATTLE

*This one is for my love, Kate: the girl who digs much of the
same sounds as I, whose eagle eyes often spot hip stuff at junk
shops well before I do, and who, when the spirit moves, can
still do an impressive Beatle Dance.*

Printed in the United States of America
Published by Sasquatch Books
Distributed by Publishers Group West
15 14 13 12 11 10 09 08 07 06 05   6 5 4 3 2 1

Cover photograph: Elke Van de Velde / elkevandevelde.com
Book design: William Quinby

Library of Congress Cataloging-in-Publication Data

Blecha, Peter.
   Rock & roll archaeologist : how I chased down Kurt's Stratocaster, the "Layla" guitar,
and Janis's boa / Peter Blecha.
     p. cm.
   ISBN 1-57061-443-1
   1. Experience Music Project. 2. Rock musicians—Collectibles. 3. Rock music—
Collectibles. I. Title: Rock and roll archaeologist. II. Title.

ML3534.B6317 2005
781.66'075—dc22

                                                                    2005049790

Sasquatch Books
119 South Main Street, Suite 400 / Seattle, WA 98104 / (206) 467-4300
www.sasquatchbooks.com / custserv@sasquatchbooks.com

CONTENTS

▲ One of the first electric guitar amps ever marketed: an ultrarare 1933 Dobro All-Electric Amplifier.

ACKNOWLEDGMENTS

I t took a deep "collection" of pals and peers to help unearth and/or verify dusty old memories about various incidents recounted in the pages that follow—and I owe them all a big debt of gratitude for their friendship and enthusiasm for this endeavor.

Because a crucial part of successful collecting is based on positive relationships with sources, I'll acknowledge a few of the premier collectors (and/or dealers) of musical rarities—including Chris Chatman (Los Angeles), George Gruhn (Gruhn Guitars, Nashville), Gary Johnson (Rockaway Records, Los Angeles), J. Kastor (Psychedelic Solutions, New York City), Timm Kummer (Mars Music Center, Fort Lauderdale), Billy Miller and Miriam Linna (Norton Records, New York City), Kurt Nauck (Nauck's Vintage Records, Spring, Texas), Ted Owen (Bonham's, London), Greg Shaw (Bomp Records, Burbank, California), and the helpful online community at the Record Collectors Guild—with whom I've done business and/or enjoyed comparing notes over the years.

It's also been a keen pleasure to cross paths with a number of the Pacific Northwest's craziest collectors/curators, including unforgettable characters like Larry Reid, Danny Eskenazi, Ruby Montana, Milo Johnstone, and Paul Dorpat. I also salute a few of my fellow Pacific Northwest–based "vinyl junkies" who've stalked some of the same hunting trails as I: Lloyd Davis, John DeBlaiso (recordshowsof america.com), Rob Frith (Neptoon Records, Vancouver, British Columbia), Kerri Harrup, Don Kirsch, Jeff Miller (Wiley's Golden Oldies, Tacoma), Craig Moerer, Rob Morgan, Jerry Osborne *(DISCoveries* magazine), Bob Pegg, Don Rogers, Bruce Smith, John Tefteller, Neal Umphred, and Win Vidor (Positively 4th Street, Olympia).

Other helpful people include the following retail aces: Russ and Janet Battaglia (Fallout Records); Kits and Brenda Fillipi (Fillipi Book & Record Shop); Nils Bernstein (Rebellious Jukebox); Hugh Jones, Dick Potts, Scott McCaughey, Eric Lindh, Scott Farley, and the entire gang at Cellophane Square Records; Helene and Johnny Rogers (Rubato Records); Tyke and Morrie Kuhlmann (M&L Records), Dave Voorhees (Bop Street Records); and the spirited people at Cranium Records, Easy Street Records, Jive Time Records, and Sonic Boom Records.

Some of the top local collectible-poster experts I've enjoyed dealing with are Scott McDougall, Dave Faggioli, and Steve and Anne Delph (Innervisions). Some of my favorite local guitar "nuts" include Jake Sturgeon (Jake's Appliances), Rick King (Guitar Maniacs), Danny Mangold (Danny's Music), Jay Boone (Emerald City Guitars), Jim Hilmar, Joe Vinikow (archtop.com), and Mike Smith and the crew at the Trading Musician shop. Individuals at a few local labels that always supported my archiving efforts are Tom and Ellen Ogilvy at Seafair-Bolo Records; Jerry Dennon at Jerden Records; Bruce Pavitt and Jonathon Poneman at Sub Pop; and Nasty Nes, Ramon Wells, and Sir Mix-A-Lot at NastyMix Records.

I also want to acknowledge former bosses and co-workers who toiled at the same retail shops as I, including Kevin Boyle, Jeff Cox, and Laura and Mary at Budget Tapes & Records; Ben Daniel, John Ramsey, and others at Peaches Records; Dean Silverstone, Gordy Arlin, Doug Sandhop, Mike Wideen, Howard Cooper, and others at Golden Oldies; and Bob Jeniker, Paul Hansen, Tim Midgett, Tom Azure, Michael Cox, and others at Park Avenue Records. And, going way back, I thank *all* former bandmates—especially Steve Ahlbom, who penned the clever lyrics to our New Wave–era song, "You Collect," and Eric Sholund, who also helped forge the concept of the Northwest Music Archives two decades ago.

A quick nod of respect here to some of the music critic/authors—including Robert Christgau, Charles R. Cross, Jim Dawson, Paul DeBarros, Howard DeWitt, Denny Eichhorn, Clark Humphrey, Dave Marsh, Craig Morrison, Charles Shaar Murray, Robert Palmer, Dave Satzmary, and Richie Unterberger—whose work has been an inspiration, and with whom I've enjoyed conversations about various aspects of music and/or history over the years.

Next, a heartfelt word of thanks to my helpful friends at Washington DC's Smithsonian Institute, Nashville's Country Music Hall of Fame, Memphis's Blues Foundation, and Cleveland's Rock and Roll Hall of Fame. Lasting gratitude goes out to Paul Allen and Jody Patton for giving me the opportunity to contribute to the making of Seattle's music museum, Experience Music Project—and to former teammates who helped make my years there fun, particularly Bob Scheu, Sonia Heiman, Jim Fricke, Susan Pierson-Brown, Jacob McMurray, Marsha McGuire, Max Cameron, Suzanne Demers, Lynn Brackpool, Anita Gross, Stanley Smith, Ann Farrington, Julie McCauley, Constance Rice, Dawn Higgins, Julie Chesledon, Fred Silber, Heidi Rademacher, Andrea Weatherhead, Diane Andolsek, Jon Kertzer, Chris Bruce, Paige Prill, Richard Larson, John Seman, Kara Costa, Bryan Yates, Kay Ray, Laura Labate, Julie Mullaney, Char Easter, Mickey Brady, Rob Nyberg, Arni Adler, Jen Wolfe, and so many others—not to mention Janette Rosebrook, Kirsti Scutt Edwards, and Michele Wallace, who graciously assisted our recent efforts to access various artifact photographs for this book.

And, finally, I wish to acknowledge my editor at Sasquatch Books, Terence Maikels, for it is *truly* due to his vision that this memoir about a multi-decade odyssey in the nutty realm of collecting even exists. Thanks again, Terence, for this opportunity to rummage through the old memory banks—and thanks also to the book's project editor Kurt Stephan, graphic designer Bill Quinby, and all the other talented people at Sasquatch for efforts above and beyond the call of duty!

INTRODUCTION

One might reasonably expect that after a few decades of actively digging up vintage musical rarities—old records, sheet music, dance and concert posters, and instruments—as I've done, the "thrill of the hunt" would eventually wear off. Especially considering the trend toward diminishing returns for all the effort that I (and plenty of fellow collectors) noticed by the early 1990s. It seemed that the "glory days" of such collecting had passed, that the flow of cool stuff into the collectibles marketplace had slowed to a trickle, that most of the worthy collectibles had been snapped up and locked into collections.

And that shortage, coupled with a profusion of price guidebooks (and the related increase in the numbers of knowledgeable collectors), was causing values to go through the roof. Indeed, by 1984, I bemoaned in a *Seattle Times* piece about record collecting that the days of finding 29-cent used records at the Goodwill or Salvation Army thrift shops were over. But neither rising prices, nor dwindling supplies, nor increased competition could dissuade us fanatical collectors.

So we plodded on, enjoying the hobby and reveling in occasional great finds.

Then, around 1996, an unforeseen marketplace force jolted the established collectibles world, upsetting the balance of that "ecosystem" and blowing the doors wide open to a new Golden Era of collecting: the revolutionary emergence of online auction services like eBay. Collectors today can't even imagine the pre-eBay world anymore—a world where legions of dedicated collectors quietly scoured our favorite haunts and considered it a success if we randomly stumbled across some item we'd long been keeping an eye out for; a world where compiling want-lists and comparing them with dealers' stock-lists *occasionally* led to a find; a world where we figured that someone somewhere probably had just the objects we sought, but neither of us had any direct way of finding each other and making a deal.

Now, that has all changed. In fact, the swell of collectibles into the marketplace signaled an earth-shaking phenomenon that continues. That being said—and as someone who actually relished the "dirty work" entailed in slogging through cold, dank basements or stifling hot, cob-webbed attics with only a hope of discovering some interesting object as a reward—I confess that it does feel a bit strange to extol the adventureless technique of collecting via a computer console.

But, hey, you gotta go where the action is. And online auctions are proving to be the most efficient means for a seller to find a buyer for some item that would never sell at a garage sale or junk shop. Conversely, collectors can now abandon the old hit-or-miss method and instead systematically search for items that they'd previously had little hope of ever lucking across.

Buying and selling online has been nothing but extraordinarily positive and has changed the collectibles world forever. Take my first eBay encounter a few years back, for example. For my debut effort I decided to test the auction site by seeking the impossible—a seemingly mythical item that other collectors and I had been trying to turn up for decades. I typed into eBay's search engine information intended to locate a fabled 45 record: the original 1956 pressing of Bonnie Guitar's first country hit, "Dark Moon"—as allegedly issued by the small-time Malibu-based Fabor Records company prior to being licensed to Dot Records, who then promoted it into a bona fide Top-10 smash in 1957. Imagine the jaw-dropping shock when my inaugural eBay search query ("bonnie moon fabor") instantly produced an exact match. Popping up right there on the monitor was an auction lot listing for a "mint condition" copy of the legendary "Dark Moon" Fabor label single. The opening bid was four dollars, and the deadline was only two hours way. Wow, that was sure easy! With the clock ticking, I registered for an eBay account, and as the auction's close approached the bidding began. And I was, understandably, not alone in wanting the disc. But two hours later, after a furious round of bidding, I was suddenly $225 poorer—and the proud new owner of a record that brought a fresh sense of accomplishment. Although this method of acquiring a record was new to me—and sure didn't provide any of the physical joys of hunting and gathering—there was the reward of finally checking that item off of my long want-list. And later, when it arrived in the mail, I took undeniable pleasure in unwrapping it, seeing it for the first time, touching it, *smelling* it, spinning it, and then filing it away.

In the years since that fateful day I've engaged in more than 500 such online transactions. It is a very effective way to build or augment a collection, but it does lack at least one aspect of the old method of collecting: the random-chance factor . . . the possibility that you might actually discover something rare that you didn't even know existed. And that hope of being surprised by some mysterious find has long kept a lot of us involved in the hunt.

The thrill of the random-chance discovery definitely explains why I'd quickly lost interest when my parents tried to coax me into collecting coins (and then later, postage stamps). It took no time at all to realize that both coins and stamps were manufactured by the millions: if one scoured long enough, it was relatively easy to complete standard sets by inserting them in those orderly little books. But, where in that mundane check-it-off-the-list type of hobby was the real challenge or room for genuine discovery?

How, I wondered, was I supposed to get excited about beginning to collect a class of objects that a zillion other numismatists and philatelists had such a formidable head start on? Even as a lad I'd quickly deduced that the odds were horribly long that I would ever actually turn up some truly treasured coin or stamp: one that sparked a tingling sensation that something "important" had just been uncovered or perhaps even a tiny feeling that, yes, "history" had been salvaged. And so, while I was predisposed to collecting as an activity, it took me awhile to settle in and find a niche where hopes of making such finds were not such a discouraging improbability.

That's how this budding collector eventually embarked on a path of gathering old musical artifacts. It was a route that seemed to naturally lead, step by step, from being a music fan to musician to music journalist: from being a casual record collector and history buff, to amateur musicologist and cultural anthropologist, and, finally, to "rock 'n' roll archaeologist" (as I've been described elsewhere). It's been in that role that I've enjoyed a career that has included leading the development of two major recorded sound archives; helping establish a prominent music museum; meeting many of my biggest musical heroes; uncovering some of the coolest music-related objects on the planet; and experiencing the magic of handling historic instruments formerly owned by iconic musicians like Hank Williams, Chuck Berry, Bob Dylan, Roger McGuinn, Jimi Hendrix, Eric Clapton, Eddie Van Halen, and Kurt Cobain.

Now, I'm a collector who believes that—unlike the amassing of common coins and stamps—there is a real significance in the preserving of artifacts related to a vibrant cultural expression like music. And that's because, once collected, the former's original function has been thwarted. Like butterflies affixed to a board, coins won't be going anywhere soon. They'll probably never be popped out and spent, and stamps will likely not be mailed. Their primary function has been effectively negated. Well, not so with vinyl records: they are *meant* to be played, and that's what we "vinyl junkies" do with them.

Still, a record's value goes way beyond mere entertainment. Even though musical records were, for the longest time, widely considered frivolous forms of fleeting pop ephemera, they are now considered a recording of our history—a reflection of our culture. These discs document the ideas, attitudes, and dreams of a people at some particular time and place. But if *misplaced*, there is a risk that we'll lose forever an irreplaceable portion of our collective cultural heritage—and even our cultural identity. (To be sure, there are plenty of historically important musical discs that are now represented by single known surviving copies—records that exist only because of the efforts of private collectors.) And a dedicated collector's higher purpose—preserving a bit of history—is often obscured by all the clichés about the sheer oddness of your classic "collector types."

Certainly over the years there have been countless jokes cracked (George Carlin's "A Place for My Stuff"), psychological theories expounded (Dr. Werner Muensterberger's *Collecting: An Unruly Passion*), books penned (John Fowles's *The Collector*, Brett Milano's *Vinyl Junkies*, and Philipp Blom's *To Have and to Hold: An Intimate History of Collectors and Collecting*), and movies made (*High Fidelity, Vinyl,* and *Ghost World*) that touch on various facets of the collecting phenomenon. Barry Levinson created perhaps the most memorable depiction of an obsessed collector in his 1982 film, *Diner*, which featured a classic scene in which the character Shrevie scorns his poor sobbing wife for having *misfiled* a rock album into his R&B section. Oh, the horror!

While some of those sources seriously examine the "whys" of collecting behavior—or as Dr. Muensterberger puts it, this "all-consuming passion"—and others poke fun at some collectors' eccentricities, what's often overlooked is the important contributions that such people can provide their community. Whether a particular collector is viewed as an indiscriminate lunatic, a discerning connoisseur, or a systematic scholar, the physical result of the activity—a unique collection—may potentially transcend its commonly regarded status as an agglomeration of random cultural detritus and earn recognition as a repository of historically important aural and/ or graphic information.

This is particularly true of a few of my other collecting interests: old posters, vintage radio playlists, band business cards, music magazines, and other related print materials. Just as records are important for their aural content, these items reveal information about design trends, marketing angles, venue histories, regional tastes, the career arcs of various bands, etc., which is quite often not documented elsewhere.

The tracking down of rare musical instruments is a joy unto itself. They can be physically graceful and awe-inspiring—or ungainly and risible. They can fall into your clutches accompanied by no background story whatsoever—or with a fully documented history of previous ownership. They can play easily and with an almost indescribably magic tone—or defy even the most seasoned musician to coax a decent note out of them. But no matter the specific circumstances, almost any interesting instrument has *some* story to tell, as it represents the ideas and dreams of some designer/maker/manufacturer (or musician) from our past, and that alone (or the effort to try and determine or understand those details) can make it a very enjoyable, and culturally worthwhile, endeavor.

Fortunately, in recent years we've seen steady growth in the number of educational or arts institutions devoted to collecting important instruments, and archiving recorded sounds and other pop culture ephemera. But for those organizations to effectively serve their highest purpose, we notoriously secretive, lone-wolf hobbyists known as collectors must cooperate with them. (And if ever there was a behavioral trait common to all typical collectors, it's a 'til -death-do-us-part relationship with their beloved collections.)

The sorry fact remains, though: when most collectors *do* part with their stuff—when they die—their collections are usually split up and disposed of in some inglorious fashion. This collector, however, long had a different plan in mind. And so, what follows is the story of my many adventures in the wild and wacky world of rock 'n' roll archaeology, tales of finding killer stuff, crossing paths with crazy characters, and, finally, achieving what once seemed like a farfetched goal: seeing my collection of treasured rarities preserved for the ages by becoming a part of a museum's holdings.

01

FOR THE RECORDS

SIREN SONGS

As a youthful rock 'n' roll fan back in the early 1960s, I found it a perfectly satisfactory experience to just wait and listen for favorite new songs whenever they randomly aired on the radio. In time, though, I realized that each hit tune seemed to have an (un)certain shelf life. It was as if songs somehow had an invisible "best before" date stamped on them and, after a few days, weeks, or months, they inevitably slipped away and no longer received any airplay.

The problem with this situation was, as I saw it, that the individual songs hadn't lost any of their allure. To my ears, whether or not a great tune was fresh or new, it was *still* great. A classic song remained just that: timeless. And, of course, as generations of music lovers before had already figured out, part of the solution to this situation was to buy your own copy of the records that you were attracted to. Thus, my initial interest in records amounted to a simple desire to have on-hand favorite radio hits that I could spin whenever and as often as desired on the ol' Philco turntable at home. But still, for those first several years, that little stack of 45s on my bedroom bookshelf wasn't really a "collection" so much as a casual accumulation. And to the extent that my modest childhood allowance allowed, I'd pick up current singles from a downtown Olympia shop, The Music Bar, which dependably stocked all the Top-40 hits then charting on local radio.

The wake-up call for me came as a minor confrontation with one of the rude facts of Industrial Age life: obsolescence. This occurred one day when I decided to buy a now-long-forgotten 45 single that had been airing on various stations a month or two prior but had since slid off the charts. As usual, I went to The Music Bar, inquired about the record, and was told that if I placed a special order for

---

◄ Previous page: An RCA phonograph spinning the first 45 ever marketed, Eddy Arnold's "Texarkana Baby."

it they could get one for me—they'd probably have it in by the following weekend. The next Saturday I showed up only to hear the manager say, "Sorry, young man, but our distributor reports back that he can no longer supply the 45 that you wanted. It's apparently *out of print*."

Out of print. Now *there* was a phrase I'd never heard before. As I came to learn, it meant that a record, which may have been issued only a few months prior, could already be unavailable for purchase. This verdict seemed unfair, not to mention stupid. Unfortunately, it was also one that I heard on several subsequent occasions.

The Big Lesson seemed to be that if you didn't jump on an interesting new 45 while it was hot, you might lose your chance—the disc could soon be considered obsolete and then discontinued by the manufacturer. This was pop music after all, and when the captains of the entertainment industry deemed some item not *popular* enough, its fate was sealed.

Although I was too young to know it, in fact nearly *all* of the recorded music produced since records had been invented in the 1890s was by this time out of print. Nearly a century's worth of historically significant recordings by early brass bands, operatic tenors, novelty whistlers, hillbilly yodelers, and jazz and blues musicians were effectively *extinct*. Indeed, this very situation had launched the first generations of record collectors, who had been actively scouring around seeking these rare 78s for years, even prior to 1948, when the 45 single was introduced.

But for this fan, what troubled me was the frustrating realization that *rock 'n' roll* 45s too could go the way of the Dodo bird. It seemed crazy that because of vagaries of the marketplace, perfectly wonderful slices of pop music history could—if individual fans didn't react swiftly enough—conceivably be lost to the mists of time. And with that realization, it occurred to me that a good record collection served not only as a library of a collector's favorite tunes, but also, in a very real way, as a cultural repository of a fleeting and ephemeral art form.

With that mind-set—one that experts say is not uncommon among collectors of every stripe—my collection took on a much greater significance. At some point a collection shifts from an accumulation of objects the collector enjoys to a physical monument to the ethic of conservation and preservation. In his *To Have and to Hold: An Intimate History of Collectors and Collecting*, Philipp Blom quotes German philosopher Walter Benjamin, who noted that "the collector 'has taken up arms against dispersal. The great collector is touched to the core by the confusion and dispersal in which things are found in this world.'" To Blom and Benjamin, the fan, in the process of trying to bring some order to the chaotic world, becomes a casual connoisseur—and the hobbyist collector effectively becomes a historical curator.

Of course, in my days of youth, I was just irked that I couldn't have the damn 45 I wanted. I was placed at the mercies of serendipity, left to hope that I might on a distant day happen across a used copy (scratches and all) of the desired disc at some garage sale or secondhand shop.

Little did I know that a few years later—and sixty miles away in the big city of Seattle—a new industry would arise in response to local marketplace demand: entire *stores* dedicated to buying and selling used records. In the meantime, my schoolyard pals and I continued to meet at recess on the playground each day, tuning in on our little transistor radios to Olympia's KGY 1240, Seattle's KOL 1300, and my favorite DJ, Pat O'Day on Seattle's AM giant, KJR 95.

This was how we discovered all the cool new tunes, including three worth mentioning here: "Wipeout," "Louie Louie," and "The Witch." The first was a song that would actually prove to have a life-altering impact on an entire generation of kids who were inspired to try and become rock 'n' roll drummers—including myself. It was the summer of 1963 when the Surfaris hit with "Wipeout," a surf-rock song with unusual drum solo–based pop hooks. So exciting was "Wipeout" that even the mere *thought* of it automatically launched me into a spell of mindless pounding. With hands, forks and spoons, pencils—anything! And on surfaces ranging from the car's dashboard, to the dining table, to my desk at school. I was often prodded by my parents to halt, which I usually did. But when they weren't around to suppress my rhythmic exuberance, I wasn't able to discipline myself quite so successfully.

Proof of that is Exhibit A: Located in my family's archives is a letter that I was impelled to write by a teacher. He was understandably at his wit's end over my percussive proclivities. The undated memo penned in my youthful scrawl reads, in part, "Dear Mother, Today I got in trouble for pounding. I have to write this letter to you for doing it. I wasn't supposed to pound with my ruler. So I have to write this letter to you. I've been very bad today. Peter." Below that I included a "P.S." followed by an arrow pointing toward a little penciled sketch of—what else?—a drum set. And below that, my poor, beleaguered mother signed in receipt of this letter: "I understand. Please try harder. Mom."

I *did* try harder. I intensified my pleas to take up drumming— a goal I achieved only after being forced to take a couple years of piano lessons. Oh God, how I hated practicing "Rudolph the Red Nosed Reindeer" and other beginner ditties when I was already a red-blooded rock 'n' roll fan! The good news was that my older sister, Margo, took mercy and agreed to teach me the three simple chords to one of the most fun rock songs ever written: the Kingsmen's infamous "Louie Louie."

The song (as I would later learn) had actually been a minor radio hit in the Kingsmen's hometown of Portland, Oregon, during the summer of 1963. But up in Washington, we didn't hear it until the early spring of 1964—after it had become the center of a nationwide scandal over rumors that the garbled vocals supposedly included "dirty lyrics." All I knew was that the song rocked enough to merit inclusion in my collection—and that after repeated spins, the singing didn't really seem to match up with any of the naughty lyrical translation notes being passed around the playground.

Late that same year, KJR began airing "The Witch" by a band called the Sonics. Though by that time I'd become a confirmed Beatlemaniac and a fan of lots of other great British Invasion hits, "The Witch" was obviously of a whole other order. It was a tune so kick-ass that KJR—in order not to offend their housewife-listener-base's sensibilities—wouldn't even air it until about three in the afternoon, after schools let out. "The Witch" (later acknowledged as a pioneer of what came to be called "punk rock") had *everything* going for it: a killer drum beat, savage garage-rock guitars, and a singer who screamed like nothing anybody had ever heard before.

I bought the 45 and played the thing darn near to death. It was the first disc I'd ever acquired whose label bore the name of a locally based company logo, Etiquette Records in Tacoma. Now, pretty much every other 45 I'd ever acquired listed New York or Los Angeles as its point of origin, so this local angle interested me: the realization that rock bands didn't necessarily all hail from distant lands like California (the Surfaris and the Beach Boys) or England (the Beatles and the Dave Clark Five).

As "The Witch" climbed into the radio stations' Top-10 playlists, the Sonics' name began to appear more and more frequently in all those teen-dance radio ads of the day. In fact, the band seemed to be booked just about every weekend at some area dance hall. And so I was all the more excited to hear one day that the band was playing for a dance that Friday at the high school gym just a few blocks away. After dinner that night, a friend and I rode our Stingray bikes over and actually met the band after they'd set up their gear on the gym's stage. Though we couldn't stay out late enough to try and hear the show, just crossing paths with them was a thrill.

Not too long after, that same neighborhood pal and I discovered another shaggy-haired teenaged rock band practicing in a basement down the block. One day while we were spying on them through

a window, the guys spotted us and waved us down. The Bootmen, it turned out, were nice guys who also had a tuff 45, "Black Widow," that had been issued by Etiquette Records—the very same local company as my heroes, the Sonics. In fact, this firm was one of those who had, in my opinion, allowed a disc (the Bootmen's) to go out of print prematurely, making it impossible for The Music Bar to special-order it.

Being just a kid at the time, only later would I come to understand the big picture—that in the early 1960s the Pacific Northwest was home turf to one of the nation's most vibrant teenage rock 'n' roll scenes. Beginning in 1959, a remarkable string of combos—like the Ventures, the Wailers, the Fleetwoods, Little Bill and the Bluenotes, Ron Holden and the Thunderbirds, and the Frantics—all cut 45s for locally based record labels who managed, with the support of KJR and other regional radio stations, to push these recordings out past our provincial borders and into international hit status. The Fleetwoods were an Olympia High School–based doo-wop trio who'd actually composed their debut hit, "Come Softly to Me," in 1958 while walking downtown on their way to shop at The Music Bar. Massive sales caused both Tacoma's Ventures and the Fleetwoods to score number 1 hits, earning them gold records.

Before long, the area's teen rhythm-and-blues (R&B) aesthetic became known as the Northwest Sound, and its practitioners

---

▲ A classic and rare 1964 Pacific Northwest garage-rock record, the Bootmen's "1,2,3,4"/"Black Widow" (Etiquette Records #10), which went out of print by about 1965.

rapidly multiplied. In an effort to get in on this new gold rush, many new labels formed, new recording studios opened, and great second-wave bands enjoyed strong local and/or national radio hits (including the Viceroys, the Dynamics, the Kingsmen, the Sonics, the Dave Lewis Trio, Paul Revere and the Raiders, and Merrilee Rush and the Turnabouts). At this period's peak, there were well over fifty major teen dances held each week in numerous armories, roller rinks, grange halls, and old ballrooms scattered across Washington and Oregon—an energetic uprising of regional youth culture that was all the more remarkable for its rapid demise. Much as dinosaurs suddenly found their existence threatened by upstart life forms, the Northwest Sound was challenged both by the freshness of the British Invasion bands and then the psychedelic sounds of those exotic Haight-Ashbury groups. The sad result was that by about 1968 *all* of the successful local recording studios, record labels, and hit-making bands were defunct. And so began some very long, lean years for Northwest rock.

Simultaneously, and with the encouragement of my drum teacher, my parents were finally persuaded to buy me that full drum set I'd so long desired. After Dad and I picked one up at Seattle's Myers Music, I practiced diligently, and soon word filtered around the neighborhood that I was getting fairly good. This talk prompted a group of older guys to come by the house one evening. They shoved a few albums into my hands—including Jimi Hendrix's *Are You Experienced* and Cream's *Disraeli Gears*—and told me to be ready to jam on the coming weekend.

That first session was a total blast for me and though the crew never evolved into a real band, I was convinced that being in a rock band was my calling. In junior high, my first band, a "power trio" named GodMother, played sets of Hendrix, Cream, and Black Sabbath tunes at our first gigs, across town at the Skateland roller rink. While attending Olympia High, I first helped form Warbucks, a group that wrote all original songs and fancied ourselves a "revolution rock" band. Then, in 1973, I fell in with some better players and we began performing proto–heavy metal music in a band called Valhalla.

With each of these early combos, we had our fun, played a few dances, and became better musicians. The only problem was the lack of regular opportunities to perform around town. It was obvious that the route to success would require a move up to Seattle, a much bigger city where, I was certain, great opportunities surely awaited.

Although perfectly convinced that playing rock 'n' roll *was* my future, I did still have other interests, and so I hatched a plan that would allow me to continue my education while also getting me nearer the frontlines of the music biz. After graduating from high school in 1974, I saved up paychecks from a summer job, and in September—with $1,200, my drums, a couple old guitars, clothes, books, and a "collection" of about two dozen LPs and fifty 45s—I moved to Seattle to attend the University of Washington (UW) and hopefully join some promising band.

Once there, I rented a room in the U District—a student-oriented business strip anchored by University Way along the west side of the UW campus—and registered for classes. Over the next several quarters I mainly studied art (under Jacob Lawrence), history, music theory, geology, and archaeology. These last two subjects had long been of personal interest, probably stemming from my infatuation with fossils, petroglyphs, and arrowheads. As a kid I'd loved rocks. The family's annual summer salmon-fishing trips to the tiny old towns of Neah Bay and Sekiu also afforded great opportunities for picking up all sorts of interesting fossils, and a growing collection of them spurred my father to get us memberships in the Washington Agate and Mineral Society, whose weekend rock-hounding trips helped add to my accumulation. So smitten was I with geologic history and local Native American inhabitation—the prehistoric petroglyphs preserved near Tumwater Falls just a couple blocks from my home were especially intriguing—I even opted to pass up a traditional summer camp one year in favor of the History Camp held at Olympia's State Capitol

Museum, an institution that featured a fascinating mineral exhibit displayed under an eerie and magical, color-enhancing black light.

Thoroughly entranced, I read every book on these subjects that I could find at the library, worked to ID my finds, and then, after creating a display of them, was actually awarded a few ribbons at the Puyallup Fair. Perhaps it was those experiences that taught me that the process of digging up rarities, determining what they signified, and sharing them with the public was a rewarding activity—a lesson that, in time, I would apply to plowing through "midden piles" (layered remains of inhabitation) of dirt-encrusted records and eventually developing historical exhibits about them. In the meantime, as a college student, I began volunteering on weekends with the Seattle Archaeological Society, helping to excavate ancient Native American riverbank village sites located just north of town. I was quick to make some good contacts in the archaeology world, and was having a blast doing so.

At the same time, I also discovered that the U District boasted an amazing number of used-book and used-record shops, including the Tyee Book Store, Puss & Books, Honest John's Records, Campus Music, and Cellophane Square. As a good customer I quickly got to know the individual shopkeepers, who provided favors, including discounts and freebies, and allowed me a "hold pile" for priority items that I couldn't always afford immediately. In hindsight, the pickings were amazing, as record collecting hadn't yet matured into the science it is today, what with published price guides and online databases about rarities and their values. At the time it was just good clean fun as well as an educational process—a combination that led me to broaden my searches and to discover additional good sources scattered around town (including record haunts like the Salvation Army and Goodwill thrift shops, the Music Flea Mart, Standard Records, the Fillipi Book & Record Shop, Platters, Bob's Record City, and the Ballard Record Shop), which I placed on my evolving tour itinerary.

And in such places (especially the attic of the latter) a whole new world opened up before my eyes—imagine the glorious sight of uncountable numbers of dusty old 78s from the 1920s and '30s stacked clear up to the rafters, countless LPs spilling out of wooden crates and wall racks, and vast quantities of *out-of-print* 45s. To a budding record nut, these overflowing stashes appeared as something akin to the golden riches amassed in long-lost Egyptian burial tombs.

Facing this bounty, I heard the siren song of rarities call out to me, and a lifelong hobby was kick-started. In short order I established a pattern of making my weekly "rounds"—an after-class walking tour that took me through each of these shops (and others), where I hacked away in a systematic effort to plow through these zillions of discs and, at the same time, to review each shop's newly arrived stock. This was all great fun, not the least because the going prices back then were so attractive: instead of a new LP for $5.97, it was easily possible to snag used *rarities* for anywhere between dimes and dollars. This sense of bargains-to-be-had led to much enjoyable experimentation through acquisition of weird records I'd never even heard of. Now, rather than just searching for songs that I remembered and liked, I began finding and buying *anything* that seemed interesting, including 1950s doo-wop and rockabilly singles, obscure 1960s psychedelic albums, and even records on Northwest labels that I'd never laid eyes on before.

Meanwhile, I also kept up efforts to find a band worthy of joining, leading to a long series of jam sessions in various dorms, frats, and off-campus rooming houses. I'd pushed through three years of study at the UW and I finally had to declare a major. Still leaning toward archaeology, I sought out expert advice by making an appointment with the appropriate departmental student advisor. After listening to a brief outline of my intentions, she asked, "So, then: You come from a *wealthy* family?" She was quick to inform me that being an archaeologist meant working in a low-paying field with few open positions. Worse yet, the role basically required either direct connections to deep-pocket sources or a constant effort to rustle up funding grants.

Her words were pretty discouraging, to say the least. I was already struggling to pay my way through college—not to mention financing my record-collecting hobby. There was just no way I was going to invest a ton of effort in chasing down rich patrons to sponsor whatever dig sites I might eventually become associated with. My interest was in history, not schmoozing, and this reality slap sparked an abrupt change in my goals. Dropping out of college, I decided to finally get serious about forming a band. But for the time being, I still needed a job. So I decided to see if I could snag some work at one of the U District record shops, and as luck would have it the very first one I stopped by, Budget Tapes and Records, hired me on the spot. One of the great benefits of working there was that I began befriending numerous customers who were also young musicians attempting to put bands together—although those stars still weren't quite aligned for me just yet . . .

Instead, I enjoyed the steady income and the fact that my knowledge of music was increasing exponentially—work in the shop allowed me to stay current because I heard all the new records. Even though Budget didn't deal in used or rare records, I found myself in a classic case of role reversal: a decade after I had first confronted the sad fact of obsolescence, with this job I was now suddenly the shop clerk who had to inform customers that the dated song they'd requested was now unavailable. This is how I learned, for example, that all those great oldies hits by stars such as Roy Orbison and the Dave Clark Five were already *long* out of print.

With this enhanced state of appreciation for such rarities, I was now well on my way to being a certified full-time record nut. Soon the used-record shops no longer provided an adequate stream of records to peruse—and too, the risk always existed that the shopkeepers themselves might decide to keep an incoming record for themselves or even sell it to a customer other than me. I realized I needed to work the frontline trenches. I ramped up my scouring of garage sales, thrift shops, and flea markets—anywhere that held out the hope of having records that hadn't been cherry-picked yet.

By about 1977 all this scouring for rare records had taught me two things: first, that all those local stars like the Kingsmen and the Sonics had released *a lot* of other 45s in the 1960s beyond the few I'd heard on the radio in my youth; and second, that numerous local labels had released great numbers of 45s by tons of other combos that I'd never even heard of. Most significant to me was the fact that *all* of this stuff was out of print and now represented the detritus of what amounted to a lost civilization of teen rock. Fading reminders of the glorious heyday of the Pacific Northwest's early music scene were now represented only by "archaeological" remains: 7-inch, 10-inch, and 12-inch slabs of scratchy old vinyl.

That's when I realized that these little discs were in fact records of a historical nature. Each one existed as an aural document of a long-ago recording session by an artist who had a song they believed in—coupled with high hopes that they were cutting a hit that would launch them into stardom. Indeed, I came to view each newly discovered 45 (or 78 or LP) as a valuable conduit for the passing along of information from the past. It became clear that records are much like books, of which Blom so eloquently writes, "[they] have the most powerful and subtle connotations, for they are never only objects, they have a voice with which they can speak across time and across lives."

And when records spoke to me, their message mostly offered strings of mysterious riddles: *Who* are these long-gone singers and musicians? *When* did all this regional recording activity begin? *Who* ran all these obscure local record companies like Rainier, Evergreen, and Morrison Records? *Where* did they record this stuff? And *why* did those earlier music scenes fade away, leaving little trace in recorded history? Little could I have known then that my ensuing efforts to dig up all this buried "lost history" would become a decades-long pursuit.

THE FEVER

By the late 1970s, one measure of how far down the path I'd already stumbled toward becoming a full-fledged record-collecting fanatic was that for three whole summers while traveling the country working as an Amtrak train porter, my top priority was rummaging through used-record shops—this instead of grabbing some desperately needed sleep in each layover town (as fellow porters did). That's how those precious few hours of personal time were spent in places like Chicago, Minneapolis, Vancouver, British Columbia, Eugene, Oakland, Los Angeles, and Salt Lake City (though the last town proved to be the one place I could never find what I was looking for).

While making my usual rounds when back home in Seattle, I was also crossing paths with a growing circle of other collectors, each of whom seemed to have their own areas of interest: the Beatles, Elvis, doo-wop, rockabilly, psychedelic music, punk, and so on. But what we *all* had in common was the fever to dig out more and more records. And what kept most everyone at it was the buzz attained in the hunt . . .

When you scout for musical collectibles, and your sixth-sense antennae registers that some particular junk shop or garage sale may have some vinyl awaiting, the excitement upon approach builds to a fever pitch. Your eyes narrow, surveying the scene like an eagle tracking the movement of a field mouse. An internal monitoring system begins to scope out any nearby competition. Instinct and experience combine to give off an aura of casualness so as to not tip off any witnesses to your state of agitation. Then you close in for the kill. And once the targeted prey is bagged, there comes an adrenaline rush, a heady feeling that, once again, you have scored a big trophy specimen. Though you're high as a kite for the moment, that triumphal buzz will all too soon wear off, and the whole cycle begins again.

Considering these intense reactions and responses so common to collectors, it's plain to see why experts have long noted the apparent parallels between the behaviors of individuals who collect and those who have drug dependencies. University of Utah's Professor Russel W. Belk has (according to a University of Toronto–associated material cultures Web site) even observed that "like those who are addicted to chemical substances, the collector also undergoes 'altered states of consciousness' produced through" their hunting and collecting activity. Indeed, of world-class collectors—no matter their areas of interest—*Kirkus Reviews* has observed that "the one certain rule that governs them all is that they reach no saturation point: Collecting is the addiction par excellence." Perhaps most appropriately, as critics have tried to tar us collectors with links to drug addiction, the moniker "vinyl junkie" has been happily adopted by many of us.

While there is certainly plenty of room for poking fun at record collectors and their eccentric ways, every year there are more and more of us crawling through spiderwebs and over rusty nails in a frenzied search for more vinyl—especially in the two decades since CDs were introduced, essentially bringing the vinyl-record era to an end. In fact, looking back, by about 1978 the ranks of record collectors were growing so quickly that Seattle/Tacoma had already become the site of an annual record collectors convention.

Like any other type of trade show, the annual meet-ups consisted of a public hall with sellers and buyers gathering around tables or booths, in this case crammed with records and other music memorabilia. The spirited bartering, bargaining, and arguing recalled a primitive town's marketplace. And this noise—along with the clash of tunes emanating from a multitude of competing record players, all testing out new finds—would probably make the fabled cacophony at the Tower of Babel seem pleasant. Perhaps the greatest lesson in such gatherings was an ancient one: that one man's trash truly is another's treasure.

And with all that "trash" being offered, most of us junkies could count on going away at the end of the annual show with a stack or two of priceless "treasures." For me, this was an easy goal to meet because my musical curiosity and collecting interests were rapidly expanding. By the late 1970s, my collection had grown to about three hundred 45s and six hundred LPs.

Part of this growth resulted from a renewed interest in the musical genius of Jimi Hendrix. Up until his death in 1970, Hendrix had released only four legitimate albums. But his final years (and those after his death) had been plagued by a flood of bootleg albums that were sold on the black market. On the one hand, these illicit LPs were an unfair breach of Hendrix's record label and estate's rights to control, and profit from, music only they had the legal authority to market. On the other hand, many master tapes of classic concert performances by Hendrix weren't owned by these two parties. Without the bootleg trade, many of us prime fans would never, ever, have had the chance to hear a few more precious notes by our departed guitar hero.

It was this second consideration that first had me dabbling in Hendrix bootlegs. After realizing the bounty of music they contained, I went full tilt, scooping up anything associated with Seattle's most famed rock artist. Within a few years, my Hendrix collection had probably surpassed thirty LPs and twenty-five 45s.

The other reason that my collection had been expanding was that after a decade of relative hibernation, the Northwest rock scene was once again starting to show a few signs of life. It was around 1976–77 that a new generation of musicians—weaned on old Sonics records and inspired by new punk pioneers like New York's Ramones and England's Sex Pistols—formed bands like the Tupperwares, the Meyce, and the Mentors. And in true DIY style, a few bands—like the S'nots and the Telepaths—independently recorded and released 45s that were sold on a consignment basis in U District shops.

Fascinated by this sudden resurgence of scrappy rock 'n' roll entrepreneurialism (and excited by these bands because some were my customers at Budget), I was inspired to make a clean break with profitable employment in order to force myself to get in a band and finally get my drumming career under way. In the years after quitting Budget, I began jamming and/or auditioning with various local punk or New Wave groups—including the Macs Band, the Moberlys, the Connections, the Vacuumz, the Young Executives, the Test Animals, Zero Deals, and Face Ditch—before finally running out of savings and reluctantly accepting a position with Desire, a money-making Top-40 club act that played rooms all across the state and into Montana and Alaska.

The problem was that Desire played oldies rather than originals, and so in late 1979 (having banked considerable funds) I quit, took on a part-time job at a new U District store, Peaches Records and Tapes, and set about looking for fellow players who wanted to create original music. And the town's record-store scene was the perfect place to meet fellow musicians, as it seemed that just about every shop clerk, and half our customers as well, were already in a band or trying to put one together. Discount Records had Jeff Cerar, who played with the Cowboys; Fallout Records employed Tom Price of the U-Men; Cellophane Square hired a fun newcomer to town named Scott McCaughey, who led the Young Fresh Fellows to fame (and now plays with R.E.M.); in time Peaches would provide employment to a couple guys from the Posies and Mark Lanegan of the Screaming Trees; and Park Avenue Records had Tim Midgett of Silkworm.

Meanwhile, in early 1980 I auditioned with a promising band called the Debbies (who had just been touted in a cover feature in the *Seattle Weekly* as the town's "next big thing"). I was mightily impressed by the quality of the songs we ran through—indeed, I could hardly believe that these guys had actually penned them all. I heard any number of potential hits among the set, and when asked, readily agreed to join on.

Over the next year, the Debbies played every dark, dank, punk room from Seattle to Portland, Tacoma to Bellingham, before cutting a few (unreleased) recordings and then finally fizzling out. Over much of the next decade I would perform with a string of other good bands—Concordia Discors, the Musical Chairs, Me, and the Chains of Hell Orchestra among them—and they all pretty much followed a similar path, some actually issuing records. Three songs were even issued by the fledgling Sub Pop a few years before that label hit its stride with the grunge era. But none of the groups ever scored that glorious smash hit we all longed for. As that axiom informs: Those who fail to create hit records are fated to collect them.

GOLDEN OLDIES

In early 1982 I was momentarily between bands and so found myself mixing sound at shows of some friends' new band. It was one of these nights, at a downtown loft dance-party gig, that I met a pretty blond graphic designer named Kate. As she was also a musician, we hit it off immediately and six years later would marry. In the meantime, we both enjoyed spinning records and dancing around the apartment we soon shared, as well as going out and hearing as much live music as possible.

Usually this meant going out to see rock bands, but for guilty pleasures we also indulged in checking out all the smoky piano bars, where we'd have a few drinks and cynically request worn-out pop standards from our piano man. We watched the aging crowd's gleeful reactions when Lou Bianchi (at the Tradewinds), Howard Bulson (at Sorry Charlie's), or Dick Dickerson (at the Dog House) would launch into, say, "I'll Take You Home, Kathleen" (the song that had inspired Kate's birth name), or maybe something perfectly moronic like "Bicycle Built for Two." And as the assembled squares would revel in memories as they sang along, we would snicker evilly to ourselves.

But we also met some very nice people at those nightspots, singing along and dancing to the old, old tunes. One particular couple in their sixties, Mickey and Marvin, struck up a conversation over a few cocktails, informing us how they too loved music. We learned that they even had a rec room replete with a wet bar, billiard table, pinball games, neon beer signs, and jukebox stuffed with 45s.

Marvin said he thought we'd really like the music in their jukebox, as it featured just the same sort of pop "classics" that he'd heard us requesting from Dickerson. As the evening wore on, they insisted we stop by their place the next day and check out their basement bar. I was hesitant until Marvin, after learning that I was a record collector, sweetened the deal by offering to let me pick through the crates of old 45s they had stacked in their garage. Marvin had known a jukebox vendor back in the 1950s, and for years that friend had brought him boxloads of discs whenever he updated the stock in the various tavern jukeboxes that he serviced around town. And, because this couple's tastes leaned toward the pop end of the music spectrum, they didn't like that noisy rock 'n' roll or R&B stuff at all. In fact, anything with electric guitars, saxophones, or drums—all that 1950s rock 'n' roll and R&B "junk"—had been consistently exiled as unsuitable for their jukebox. Thirty years later, these rejects were still quarantined out in the garage.

When we accepted their invitation and dropped by, Marvin played the gracious host, making a round of cocktails, giving us a tour of his party pad, and then finally dragging the crates of reject records out for examination. I opened the first crate and was simply stunned. Never before in all my years of record hounding had I beheld such a sight. I felt like the vinyl-junkie equivalent of Howard Carter entering King Tut's tomb in 1922 and discovering mounds of priceless golden treasure. Here in the basement of an unprepossessing middle-class home on Seattle's Beacon Hill, I had lucked into unearthing a veritable time capsule of *hundreds* of quite rare 45s. A stash of unloved early rock 'n' roll discs had been shunted off by their owners so that the home jukebox could make room for all those Doris Day and Perry Como singles.

So it was that I had the thrilling experience of laying eyes for the very first time on examples of legendary Holy Grail labels from New York and Los Angeles's golden era of doo-wop—the kinds of records that *never* seemed to turn up in Seattle. In my hands I held specimens I'd only ever heard about, songs I'd only ever heard on latter-day compilation LPs. Here were classics issued by Aladdin Records, Doo-tone Records, End Records, Flair Records, Gone Records, Gotham Records, Onyx Records, RPM Records, Winley Records, and many more. I had never heard of many of the groups, but what I *did* know was that all these discs were certain to either contain raucous rock 'n' roll guitar playing (or drumming) or black doo-wop singing. And that the cost to be educated about all these recordings was just right: they were being offered to me for *free*. It was a windfall of vintage vinyl: musical manna from Heaven.

In one fell swoop, my formerly modest collection of oldies was instantly fortified into a formidable library of quite valuable classics. More significantly, I was suddenly in possession of a stunning stockpile of "trade bait"—and I wasted little time in hauling a few that weren't keepers around to barter with various dealers in order to get records that I *did* want.

At that time one of the best trading posts was Golden Oldies, a little hole-in-the-wall in a dilapidated garage over on Roosevelt Way in the U District that I happened across in the summer of 1983. The place was run by Dean Silverstone—a *real* character whom I recalled as the former host/promoter for the old *Northwest Wrestling* TV show, and who now specialized in used 45s. By aggressively stocking up on many hundreds of thousands of them, he'd successfully managed to carve out a market niche unique to the area.

Still, it's fair to say that even with all his stock, it was not every day, or week, or month, or year that someone strolled into his shop with the kind of records I was now bringing in to trade. Dean played it cool, eyeing me up and down, trying to figure out who and where I was coming from with such killer stuff, but I coyly resisted offering much info to help him out and we proceeded to do some mutually beneficial trading for the next few weeks.

But then Kate, bless her heart, pointed out that since my last band had broken up, I didn't have any sort of steady income rolling in. And that realization led her to note that I needed to think about getting a new revenue stream, or as she so efficiently phrased it: "a job." And so it came to pass that one day in September 1983 I walked into Golden Oldies and asked Dean if he thought he could use some help around the shop. From others, I already knew that Dean was considered the town's rare-45 guru, and over time as his employee I would learn that he was also an excellent teacher who could provide me with an advanced training course in the professional arts of evaluating, buying, and selling vinyl rarities.

► The rare original 1963 issue of the Kingsmen's "Louie Louie" 45.

ARCHIVAL ACTION 02

LOUIE LOUIE
(Richard Berry)

(JD-30)
Limax Music
(BMI)
Time 2:42

THE KINGSMEN
712

RADIO WAVES

As the 1980s rolled by, I continued to play drums in rock bands and work at Golden Oldies. It was here that I experienced a few of the classic retail incidents that remain vivid memories. Like the time when this guy showed up with a couple of skanky stripper gals in tow, selected a stack of cassettes, and pulled out his charge card, which showed me that he was the namesake son of Seattle's famous Mafia boss. Or the time when a calm middle-aged fellow surprised me by purchasing a rare heavy metal LP by the band Coven for $25. I asked if he wanted a bag for it; he said "no need" while simultaneously snapping it in two on the counter's edge, inquiring nicely if I'd toss it out for him, and quipping that he was merely doing what he could to keep "Satanic" records away from kids. Or the day that a buck-naked man—painted royal blue from head to toe and wielding a butcher knife—walked up and was just reaching for the door when I slammed the lock shut and called the cops.

Dealing in secondhand merchandise (like used records) also, of course, carries the risk of handling hot property. One such incident, which occurred a few years later when I was working at the Park Avenue Records shop, was a stone classic. One evening, I received an alarming phone call at home from my pal, Barry Curtis, the organist with the Kingsmen. He was upset that his house had just been burgled and wanted me to know that among the things stolen had been both his prized gold record awards for the band's 1963 hit single, "Louie Louie," as well as their follow-up album. Indeed, to add insult to injury, the thief had actually pried the gold discs out from their vintage frames, causing considerable physical damage. It was sad news; I assured him that I'd keep my ears to the rail listening for any sign of those discs popping up on the collectors market. Well, a full year went by, and then one day a scabby, disheveled fellow showed up at the shop seeking to sell off a box full of records. I plowed through them preparing to make an offer, and toward the bottom

24

I came across a wad of crumpled newspapers wrapped around something mysterious. Unwrapping that package, I made the heart-stopping discovery of two gold-covered "Louie Louie" records—both sans frames. Quickly connecting the dots, my boss Bob Jeniker jotted down information from our seller's ID cards and proceeded to slowly write him a company check for the items while I called Curtis to tell him the good news. Long story short: Curtis raced over and was happily reunited with his records. Although the thief had fled, we contacted the police and he was subsequently arrested. Ah, the joys of working the front lines of retail.

Meanwhile, my collection was growing by leaps and bounds. Now numbering more than five thousand items, it included a museum-quality collection of locally published sheet music dating back to the 1880s; records by several of Seattle's and Portland's top dance orchestras of the Roaring Twenties (these were cut by mobile field teams traveling up and down the West Coast, and then issued by major New York and Los Angeles labels); numerous 78s cut since the 1940s at the Northwest's first pioneering studios; and every other disc recorded and issued by local artists up to the present that I had been able to find so far.

My search for vinyl had taken me to locales ranging from tiny Oregon coastal towns, where I stopped in at random podunk radio stations in a quest to strike up conversations with old DJs; to trawling expeditions with Kate, under the guise of "vacations"; through just about every hamlet in all of Eastern Washington that ever had a radio station or music shop. And though I didn't always come away with great finds, the frequency with which I did pull a winner out of the dusty record stacks at some rural barn sale or church bazaar was plenty high enough to keep me at it. You just could never know where or when true gems would be dragged out. Much as you have to stare at the ground while seeking arrowheads, you often had to look at a lot of worthless stuff before you spotted the real deal among the dross.

In addition, I made the most of this traveling by conducting information-gathering interviews with old-timers whenever it seemed promising. And within a few years this ongoing effort resulted in an accumulation of more than two hundred taped oral-history interviews with nearly all of the important figures from the Northwest's early music scene. Besides the veteran label owners, engineers, and DJs I'd corralled into sessions, I also bagged interviews with every local hit-making star I could locate, including Bonnie Guitar, Dave Lewis, the Barons, the Gallahads, the Fleetwoods, the Frantics, the Wailers, Ron Holden, the Ventures, the Dynamics, the Viceroys, the Kingsmen, the Sonics, Little Bill and the Bluenotes, Merrilee Rush and the Turnabouts, and Paul Revere and the Raiders, plus many, many other fine musicians.

What a thrill it was to first meet the talents behind all those radio hits I'd loved as a kid—records that had been produced locally and then promoted into regional, national, or even international hits. And it was a pleasure as well to have these people graciously give their time and attention to a fan and mere record-store clerk whose enthusiastic dreams for a regional music museum must have sounded at least a little naïve. Whether or not they believed that such a thing was possible I don't know, but every last one of them supported my efforts, and in doing so helped nurture my big dream.

It was in late 1986 that I pitched an idea to a guy at Seattle's top local oldies station, KVI-570: do a program highlighting Northwest rock 'n' roll. Luck struck again and, as a freelance co-producer, I was soon writing a ten-hour radio special based on my record collection and a fresh series of recorded studio interviews conducted with most of the stars mentioned above. By March 1987, KVI was promoting "The History of Northwest Rock" show as no less than "literally the first serious attempt at chronicling . . . the development of the original Northwest Sound."

Media response was favorable. After the show aired, both KVI and I received an avalanche of supportive comments from the listening public, and a month or so later the station actually rebroad-cast all ten segments. Our local community *did* have an interest in its history after all, and I became ever more determined to publicize the worth of our region's music and entertainment-industry history.

Picking up on the trend, a group of local music-industry figures announced the formation of a nonprofit trade and advocacy group called the Northwest Area Music Association (NAMA). Their stated goal was "to promote national awareness of the Northwest's thriving music scene, and to provide a centralized network for regional professionals." They published a directory of most every local company that was at all related to the needs of musicians—record stores, recording studios, graphic designers, publishers, labels, clubs, sound and lighting firms. In addition, NAMA held a Music Business Conference at the new Washington State Convention and Trade Center (where, as a member of NAMA's Hall of Fame Committee, I mounted a Northwest Hall of Fame exhibit) and launched an annual NAMA Awards Show, which tallied the public's votes and awarded musicians with honors at big concert/events that became great opportunities to see performances by promising new artists like Kenny G, Sir Mix-A-Lot, and Alice in Chains. NAMA's emergence was a promising sign that Seattle's still-too-sleepy music biz was now getting more proactive at promoting itself.

IF I KNEW THEN WHAT I KNOW NOW

Behavioral experts have noted that many typical collectors seem to start with one particular goal, and then—getting caught up in the mania—they branch off into other collecting areas. In my case, what began years back as a natural attraction to a few radio hits that happened to be of local origin, became a much broader interest. Once I started to dig up previously unknown recordings by obscure musicians that had been issued decades earlier by long-forgotten record companies, I developed a raw curiosity about the breadth and depth of the Pacific Northwest's *entire* recording history. It seemed that every mysterious record I was finding—whether or not the music was worth listening to—still represented another piece of the untold story of local music.

It was obvious that up until now I'd only scratched the surface of local-music history and that in order to really learn what had transpired I would have to focus more on conducting primary research. I would need to go directly to the best available sources—additional veteran musicians and other figures who had been involved in the local music scene—and try and pry information out of them.

The first research area was determined by my love of Jimi Hendrix's music, a deep curiosity about what the Seattle native's local musical roots were, and a coincident bit of frustration with the fact that all of the Hendrix biographies thus far published seemed to share a distinct lack of information about his first eighteen years of life—the Seattle years. Especially the years in the late 1950s and early 1960s when he first took up the electric guitar, when he'd joined his own first teen bands, and when he wrote his first songs.

The first Hendrix book, Chris Welch's 100-page *Hendrix: A Biography* (1973), had devoted exactly ten paragraphs to Jimi's formative years. Three years later, and at twice the length, Curtis Knight's 222-page *Jimi: An Intimate Biography of Jimi Hendrix* offered about the same quantity of detail. Then, in 1978, David Henderson's *Jimi Hendrix: Voodoo Child of the Aquarian Age* provided only about 17 out of 384 pages on the topic.

It dawned on me that if Hendrix had been what loads of critics, peer musicians, and my own ears had told me was true—that is, an instrumental genius and by far the finest electric-guitar player the universe had yet seen—it might just be worthwhile knowing the who, what, where, when, and why of his musical education. Many a music scholar had spared no effort to research and understand these five

W's about the emergence of other notables, ranging from Mozart to McCartney. Yet with Hendrix, it seemed nobody really knew anything of importance about his earliest interests in music. Obvious questions included: Did Jimi grow up listening to the radio? Did he attend local high school dances? Had he absorbed any of the region's rockin' R&B aesthetic? Or did he favor any of the top local bands on the Northwest's "Louie Louie" scene? As one of the premier 1960s rock 'n' roll icons, it seemed obvious that Hendrix would have possessed an early interest in music, and that the untold saga of his local days was one worth uncovering.

Because local newspapers had periodically published articles mentioning that Jimi's family still lived in the area, and various quotes given to these newspapers by his father, Al, showed the man to be a warm and open guy, I decided to take a stab at unraveling Jimi's backstory. It was around 1978 that I first located Al Hendrix, mustered up my courage, and gave him a call. Unafraid of this stranger contacting him, he kindly invited me down to his house in South Seattle, where he generously shared memories about Jimi's early days. I learned intriguing things about their significant family history. For example, unknown to me, Jimi's grandparents had first arrived in Seattle as vaudevillian performers booked to entertain with the Dixieland Spectacle at the town's first World's Fair, 1909's Alaska-Yukon-Pacific Exposition. Al also bragged a little that back in the 1940s he and Jimi's mother, Lucille, had both been music fans and competitive dancers at various area nightclubs and ballrooms.

This family history in music and entertainment was all fascinating stuff, but my main area of interest at that meeting was Jimi's direct rock 'n' roll roots. Although I had the distinct impression that Al hadn't paid that much attention to his son's youthful activities—and really hadn't given them that much thought in the decades hence—as our discussion continued, more and more memories seemed to flow. Al recalled that young Jimi had loved listening to the music Pat O'Day aired on KJR radio, that he'd enjoyed attending all sorts of area teen dances, and that after getting his first electric guitar Jimi began writing his own songs and was soon playing in a series of local bands, including the Velvetones, the Rocking Kings, and the Tomcats.

This first of several interview sessions with Al proved to be the mother lode of biographical detail I'd hoped for. As a bonus, Al was helpful enough to actually provide me with names and telephone numbers for a few of Jimi's boyhood friends and members of his teenage bands—leads that I soon followed up on, gaining greater insights into the previously undocumented days when Seattle's most famous rocker had developed his initial love for music.

That whole experience proved to be so rewarding, both in the information I found and in the incredible people I met, that before long I realized the interview technique could also be applied to the bigger mysteries surrounding Northwest recording history. In the meantime, the collecting and studying of vintage regional records had brought about in me an ever-increasing appreciation for all sorts of long-gone musicians—a feeling that was compounded with growing intrigue over the tantalizing clues each new discovery yielded. And so, with my inner investigative historian now at full alert, I made the formal plunge and decided to dramatically widen the dragnet to include just about any old Northwest disc I came across. Now, this is not to say that I'd gone *totally* off the deep end and lost my ability to discern true quality. Given that this collecting commitment was still reined in by budgetary constraints, it remained necessary to always prioritize the acquisition of the "better" items first. But, in effect, I now no longer added items to my collection strictly based on my own listening tastes. Instead I was perceiving some level of historical value in every recording cut by a local artist or issued by a local label.

Beyond my main love for the Northwest's rock 'n' roll, R&B, and even some country-western, I was soon devouring memorabilia and records from musical styles ranging from Dixieland jazz to classical to pop. And God knows, whether in this region or elsewhere, there has always been far more of that stuff produced than rock 'n' roll and R&B. Having expanded my mission, it became easy to pick up materials, perhaps much too easy. And this was how my Northwest collection soon grew to about twenty-five 78s, eighty-five LPs, and a hundred 45s—many admittedly representing a marked decline in overall musical quality. The fact is, I now owned many records that—musically speaking—would never have made the cut and found a place in my preferred listening pile. But by *this* point, that was not *the* point. I was now consciously collecting *history*, and *every* record (including the less-than-listenable ones) had potential for providing new research leads or at least hints at whole other areas of possible inquiry.

This process was akin to Bryn Mawr College psychology professor Rob Wozniak's description of his own attraction to collecting rare books: "a combination of intellectual and personal enjoyment. It's a way of exploring the field with artifacts." In other words, Wozniak and I were both experiencing the time-tested technique of research *through* acquisition. This method justified grabbing questionable rarities now and worrying about sorting out their relative historical significance later. Certainly I was learning that this upfront investment in "mystery discs" could occasionally prove to be worthwhile. The fact is, today's researcher can't always know exactly what the true importance of some newly "discovered" item is at the immediate point of capture. Often it's only afterward, when the item can be closely observed (or, in our case, listened to)—or when additional related artifacts turn up and other clues fall into place—that some detail about it leads to answers.

Even though I hadn't yet heard of this idea and was simply operating on raw instinct, the "research through acquisition" approach just *felt* right—and that's the collecting philosophy I applied. So even though I couldn't always justify the acquisition of some obscure record on purely musical grounds—admittedly, the "normal," rational reason to buy a record—having this all-inclusive attitude proved to be correct, as some of the unknowable records I'd picked up along the way would in time, via incrementally accrued background knowledge, reveal their mysterious histories.

One good example is a remarkable acetate disc that I'd acquired at some record convention. These peculiar records are typically one-of-a-kind units originally cut so that, say, an artist or producer can study the recording overnight to determine whether or not it's of acceptable quality and thus ready for pressing and release to the public. Often the recording will be approved—but other times it's rejected and the artist returns to the studio to recut the song, perhaps with an alteration to the arrangement, lyrics, or instrumentation. In such a situation, the acetate becomes historic (and highly collectible) because it contains an alternate, and otherwise unavailable, rendition.

The acetate disc I'd acquired was a Listen Records 45 of a song called "Thunderbolt," performed by the Appeals. All I knew upon finding it was that Listen Records was a long-gone Seattle-based 1950s pop label. Any other clues were strictly based on hunches: that a band named "The Appeals" was probably something like a barbershop quartet or a cocktail lounge trio, but still, the song title, "Thunderbolt," held some promise of being a decent rock 'n' roll tune.

Upon arriving home, I spun the disc and was delighted that it was, in fact, a pretty good rock 'n' roll instrumental. *Cool.* Now there was just the question of *who* the heck were these Appeals. Luckily, by the early 1980s I had launched a new initiative to solicit interviews with a wide range of veterans from the local scene—musicians, label owners, recording engineers, club owners, radio DJs. With each session, lots of little mysteries were solved—and a ton more were uncovered. In hindsight, it was but a matter of time before this Appeals riddle was solved.

▶ An ultrarare 45, "Tired of Livin'"/"If I Knew Then" (Country Records), recorded in Seattle circa 1959 and "secretly" featuring a pre-fame Buck Owens.

As it happened, I was chasing down how one of my favorite early bands, the Viceroys, had come into existence. In the process of conducting interviews with various band members, I finally made contact with their old organist, Mike Rogers. As he regaled me with details of his joining the band—and how in 1962 they'd scored their big regional radio hit, "Granny's Pad"—we also chatted about his personal beginnings as a musician. That's when he suddenly blurted out that his very first band had been called the Appeals. My response was one word: "Thunderbolt."

Rogers was visibly thunderstruck. "Wow! *How in the world did you know that*? That was the tune we thought would be our big hit. We recorded that back around 1958 and I haven't even thought of it since!" In gratitude for solving the Appeals mystery, I made a cassette tape of the disc for Rogers and upon presenting it to him, I had the additional pleasure of watching his face light up as he heard a true flash from the past.

I had a similar experience with a certain bunch of circa 1950s country-western 45s I'd collected blindly in my pursuit of all things Northwest. All I knew when I bought them was that they had local addresses printed on their labels— like the tiny towns of Fife and Puyallup, Washington—and that, priced from a dime to a quarter, they fit nicely into my budget.

But on these particular discs the quality of the chicken-pickin' guitar work was truly intriguing. It almost sounded straight out of the Buck Owens school of country-western Fender Telecaster playing. Just a guess, but the supposition wasn't entirely out of the realm of possibility. See, I knew that Owens—by now a major national star—had lived and worked in Tacoma between 1958 and 1960, hosting his own local TV show (the *Bar K Jamboree*), which I'd watched as a young kid.

I knew of no published documentary evidence that Owens had done any recording during his Northwest years. But as I pursued the history behind Seattle's pioneering sound engineer, the late Joe Boles, his widow allowed me to photocopy their old studio log—an information-rich binder with the signatures of hundreds of musicians who had held sessions in that West Seattle basement studio. A cluster of autographs caught my eye. There, next to a word of thanks to Boles, were inscriptions by Buck Owens himself and a bunch of bandmates, including one Rollie Webber.

Aha! Rollie Webber was credited as the artist on one of the 45s in question. And taking a second look at the disc, I saw that the song "If I Knew Then" actually listed Buck Owens as the composer. This was an interesting development—but one that I had no way to follow up on.

Until, that is, many years later, when I managed to arrange an interview with Owens at his offices in Bakersfield, California. I brought a cassette tape of a few of these local recordings, and after the main interview I asked, "Oh, Buck, one last thing?" "Sure, what's that?" "I'd like you to hear a song or two that might interest you." I rolled the tape and to my astonishment, not more than a couple bars into the first song Owens waved his hand in an agitated fashion and blurted out something like *"That's* me. That's my guitar." I said, "Wait, Buck. How about this next song?" He said, "That's me, too. I remember those licks. What *song* is that? Where'd you *get* that?"

And so the encounter continued, with Owens recounting that he'd recorded a number of obscure singles during his Northwest years—*all* of them credited to other singers, such as his bassist, Webber—and *none* of them documented in existing discographies. Furthermore, he rattled off a number of other songs he'd cut while in the Northwest—but I can't reveal their titles, as the search for them continues . . .

Another benefit of gathering up 45s bearing labels that I came to associate with the local 1950s country-western scene was that I belatedly realized that on the fringes of that world there had existed a remarkable number of young rockabilly musicians. Yes, long before teenage bands in the Northwest began forging the saxophone and Hammond organ–laden sound of the "Louie Louie" era, there had actually been a full generation of early rock 'n' roll pioneers who'd taken their cue from the southern hillbilly cats like Elvis Presley, Jerry Lee Lewis, and Gene Vincent.

As I poked around by asking rockabilly collector friends what they knew about this, I came to understand that I was way behind on the topic. It seems that the well-organized fans in Europe and Japan had long ago discovered that most every region of the United States had produced a few rockabilly singers—and by this late date, a good number of these discs were recognized as real gems, at least as rare and desirable as the best stuff out of Memphis. Luckily, through persistence and luck, I managed over time to obtain recordings of all of the great rockabilly singers from the Northwest: 45s like Clayton Watson's "Everybody's Boppin'," Wally Lee's "Oh No Daddy-O," Leon Smith's "Little Forty Ford," Peggy Griffith's "Rockin' the Blues," and Sheree Scott's "Whole Lotta Shakin'."

But one other such record stubbornly refused to show up—a record that had become legendary as one of the world's most coveted 1950s rockabilly 45s, "Shake Um Up Rock," by the Benny Cliff Trio. I quietly searched for years and years with no success, and I can't even begin to describe the anguish I felt over having been so ignorant

35

about it during the years when numerous copies had popped up and were promptly sold by my dealer friends to overseas buyers at prices in the stratospheric $1,500 range. It was little comfort that I did find various *other* singles issued by the same label, Portland's Drift Records—it just pained me to no end that perhaps *the* finest example of local rockabilly music would possibly remain unattainable. And all the while, a good number of well-heeled foreign collectors already had *their* own copies safely stowed away. As someone who regularly scavenged great items for ten cents up to maybe $20 (or perhaps $60 max), it just seemed an impossibility that, even if a copy were ever offered to me, I would even be able to afford it.

But diligence finally paid off when I went on a record-hunting field trip with a pal one weekend. He'd gotten a tip about a fellow in mid-divorce who needed to sell a large collection fast. We drove to the Seattle suburb of Mercer Island, entered a double-car garage, and spent the next few hours calculating the worth of this man's collection, coming up with a wholesale offer. The sheer quantity of the records was amazing, but amid all the Annette Funicello, Beatles, and Elton John records was one that made my day: an immaculate copy of Benny Cliff's masterpiece.

My buddy knew perfectly well the legend of this 45—but he also understood my need to have it. In addition to paying me for my help in appraising the collection, and giving me as a gift the nice old 1916 RCA Victrola our seller had thrown into the overall deal, he also made me an offer on the Drift single that I couldn't refuse. And so I bit the bullet and paid the going rate of $1,500—but instead of cash, I paid in the far less painful form of trade.

One other memorable breakthrough on the collections/research front occurred while I was trying to track down information about a certain local label, Morrison Records, which appeared to be one of Seattle's earliest record companies. For years I had been casually picking up these unmistakable 78s—which, rather than being pressed in the customary black color, were made in uniquely swirled, bright, multicolor vinyl. There were, up through the 1980s, lots of them floating around the area's junk shops. In addition to admiring their visual splendor, I had taken a particular interest in the ones that featured various old-time country singers—especially one named Bonnie Tutmarc.

Now, through interviews with a few other musicians, I'd already ready learned that Tutmarc had eventually (in the 1950s, and as "Bonnie Guitar") gone on to score some national radio hits—such as 1957's lovely Top-10 smash, "Dark Moon"—thus becoming Seattle's greatest country-western star. But I wanted to know anything and everything else I could about all these many undocumented Morrison discs.

Unfortunately, even the Seattle Public Library's voluminous subject files had nothing on the subject, so for a number of years I was simply stuck awaiting the eventual emergence of any clue to help crack the mystery. Then one day I opened a newspaper to a human-interest article about an elderly local gentleman. I instantly recognized him as the fellow often seen doing elegant little solo dance routines on the sidewalk at Seattle's Pike Place Market. The brief article mentioned that this Mr. "Morrie" Morrison had been a dance teacher here in the 1920s, was a dance-hall manager in the 1930s, and had even operated his own namesake record label. I was in shock. That eccentric old man that the town had been chuckling over for *years* was the very guy I'd been looking for.

One phone call later, I'd set up my own interview with Morrison. During that interview, his story and that of Morrison Records unfolded. Way back in 1919 his wife, Alice, had composed a couple of the very first national hits to come out of the Northwest (in sheet music form), and that success had made them rather wealthy. It was the Roaring Twenties, the economy was a-go-go, and the Morrisons could afford to found a song-publishing firm, a dance school, a film company, and their own record label (complete with Seattle's first pressing plant): Morrison Records.

Over the next few months I interviewed Morrie a couple times. He was full of fascinating information about the early days of the Northwest recording industry—he'd crossed paths with all the successful local songwriters, musicians, and label operators of the day. He also was so very pleased that I had taken such an interest in his past achievements, to the extent that he eventually offered to let me pick through his stuff and take whatever interested me. So, from the *thousands* of Morrison 78s, I took one of each title (that I didn't already have) and one of each sheet-music title they'd published, along with business cards, letterhead stationery, and even a few handbills and posters from the Morrison family band's vaudeville days.

GOING COMPLETIST

Thrilled that my efforts were starting to uncover some really deep lost history, I grew ever more enamored with the region's musical past. Along the way, though, another concern arose: if this music history was as important as my hunch said it was, why did no one else seem to care about it? The fact is, during all this collecting of local music I never seemed to have any noticeable competition. Throughout the 1970s and '80s, music memorabilia was still rather easy to find (and at bargain prices). Shopkeepers all over town welcomed the sight of me waltzing through their doors, always on the lookout for items that they had no other buyers for. Many gladly held incoming material aside for me, knowing that if I didn't already have the item—or if it represented a significant upgrade in condition over one I already had—they'd make a sale. Beyond this, a few collector friends even started *giving* me their Northwest items in support.

While there was definitely a fun aspect to collecting in a field that appeared to have no other pickers working it, this lack of wider community attention to our own collective history just further sharpened my own interest. I recommitted to tracking down even more of this history—a joyous task and an enjoyable hobby, but also an activity that held out about zero promise of ever becoming the foundation for a career.

Like many a vinyl junkie before me, I learned the hard way that a record-collecting "hobby" can easily morph into a full-time obsession. Some collectors apparently are satisfied with adding to their prized stashes, learning more about their favorite artist as they go, and pretty much leaving it at that. Others, like myself, take things a big step or two further and begin to see our collections as historically important unto themselves. We so highly value what we've gleaned about these recordings—and also fret that the same information is not being tracked (or stored away for the ages) elsewhere—that we begin to see ourselves as historians, as keepers of the stories embodied by our records, as people with distinction.

To various extents, this pathological self-image is probably valid: if our chosen topic of research is one that no one else is studying, we are by definition distinct, even if no one else knows it or cares. But luckily, most of us collectors who fall into this category also enjoy doing our work in private. We prefer to quietly collect without tipping anyone else off to the great little world of whatever rarities we are fixated on—after all, who needs or wants any competition?

I sure didn't, and for years it didn't seem that I had any. By the early 1980s I had stepped up my patrolling of Seattle's various record shops, making sweeps of the U District, Capitol Hill and Broadway, and the funky Fremont neighborhood at least a couple times per week. At this point, beyond just the records, I had discovered the value of accumulating print materials related to Northwest music history: old radio play charts, concert posters and handbills, early music magazines, sheet music, and promotional photos of bands. Adding serious bulk to my collection was the fact that currently active bands, labels, radio stations, nightclubs, and promoters kept dropping off new posters and handbills that were free for the taking from these shops. Because I'd befriended the shopkeepers, they were all too happy to dump tons of incoming stuff into my collection.

Though the acquisition of these newer items lacked the thrill of the hunt, it seemed clear that if somebody didn't archive them, these materials might disappear the way the older artifacts had. In fact, when viewed as part of a historical continuum, these new items' value, at least in my estimation, rose to a worthwhile level. But the rate at which they were accumulating was epic.

At some point, while pondering the considerable time span represented by my collection, I began wondering if even at this late date it might still be possible to document the audio legacy of earlier eras by developing a definitive archive of *all* local records ever produced. This idea was a quantum leap from earlier visions I'd had for my collection. I'd already made a huge change from just keeping an eye out for, say, Sonics 45s on the Etiquette label that I didn't already have, to collecting all twenty-seven singles Etiquette issued for various bands. This new idea even went beyond just looking for a better-condition copy of the Kingsmen's "Louie Louie" (as issued by Seattle's Jerden Records) and taking an interest in all 150-plus discs released by that label.

By this point, I should state, my obsession with Northwest music history had grown beyond reason, and I was avidly gathering up any and every record produced for any and every label that was ever based in the region. The more obscure the label—such as Spokane's Sound Recording Company, Wenatchee's Julian label, and Portland's Rose City Records—the better. And so, via this gradual "mission creep," one more collector had transformed into another obsessed "completist."

Little did I know that by taking on this self-imposed task I had fallen into a couple classic traps of maniacal collecting: seriality and formality. The first is, I believe, the more frequently occurring phenomenon. Almost every record nut I know collects (one or more) *series* of things. We each wind up setting goals of, say, collecting *every* record cut by some artist, *every* song written by some artist, *every* record issued by some label, or *every* different recording of some particular song.

While at first blush this practice may seem to be a healthy way to establish reasonable parameters on what might otherwise explode into limitless acquisition of an undifferentiated *more*, making a commitment to acquire such complete "runs," "sets," or "series" of any form of collectibles (whether they be baseball cards, Avon bottles, Beanie Babies, or records) actually carries its own dangers. As Susan Stewart warns in her fine book, *On Longing*, "To play with series is to play with the fire of infinity."

I can certainly attest that by expanding my focus from items of direct interest to objects related by some abstract concept, the floodgates became difficult to close back down. The paradox is that by setting the acquisition of some finite series of collectibles as a goal, I had crossed the Rubicon and was now susceptible to thoughts of collecting all sorts of series—and that, as Stewart notes, has an additional built-in downside: "this finitude [itself] becomes the collector's obsession." No longer are we focused on the items we already possess—now it's the *missing* units we want—and true to form, the glaring gaps in these series became my own fixation.

In hindsight I see that once I'd locked into collecting in such a broad fashion, I'd gone far beyond following my original interests. I'd entered an apparently predictable phase of seeing the whole endeavor as a grander undertaking. Stewart describes the progression this way: "because of the collector's seriality, a formal 'interest' always replaces a 'real' interest in collected objects." In other words, we truly serious collectors *always*, and necessarily, find a way to justify our collecting mania by casting the effort as some greater mission—and this intellectualizing is merely an attempt to lay a legitimizing cover over our craziness.

To be sure, I first began collecting records because I liked the *music* they contained. Only later did I gradually shift to viewing this

collecting as a means of accomplishing something more meaningful than my own auditory satisfaction. And so, like other collectors
before me, I eventually developed a new rationale for my passionate
activity: in my case, appreciation for the historical research potential
the discs embodied.

Such a profound change of attitude toward collected objects
can be seen as a sort of magical transformation. Philipp Blom, in
To Have and to Hold, explains this as a form of alchemical process
that "is at work whenever a collection reaches beyond appreciating
objects and becomes a quest for meaning, for the heart of the matter." The "heart of the matter" for me was that the Pacific Northwest
had a long (if underappreciated) historical musical legacy. Enough
significant music history had occurred in the area so as to make the
numerous regional history museums here seem downright derelict
in their duties for having not collected, documented, and displayed
artifacts that represented that story. And so I became determined to
do something about this oversight.

THE NORTHWEST MUSIC ARCHIVE

Though collecting vinyl records and print materials associated
with the artists and labels that produced them can be interesting on its own, the whole seems to gain value when the
collector devises a system of organizing it all. Indeed, Susan Stewart
observes that without *some* logical physical arrangement, the individual artifacts amassed are, as a group, rather meaningless: "the
collection is not constructed by its elements; rather, it comes to exist
by means of its principle of organization."

I soon found that creating an organized card catalog was what
really provided the big-picture view of the breadth of the Northwest
recording industry's history. My cataloging "system" first took shape

as a stack of handwritten three-by-five index cards filed in a shoebox. Each card held information about a particular artist and a chronological listing of their recordings. In the beginning I knew that this effort would at the very least help with the development of definitive "discographies," or documentary listings of all the recordings cut by an artist or even by a particular producer. Over time, I saw that this system simultaneously produced what record researchers call "labelographies," or documentary listings of all the discs released by a particular record company.

A collector should never underestimate the possibility of gleaning additional valuable information just by reviewing actual discs within his or her storage area. If the discs are physically arranged in logical groupings, much can be learned just by studying them and their packaging in relationship to their contemporaries. For example, I devised a two-tier organizational approach for my collection: first dividing the discs by decade (1920s, '30s, '40s, '50s, '60s, '70s, and '80s), and then further breaking them down by genres (country, jazz, R&B, rock 'n' roll). This way I could easily physically compare and contrast what was being issued within various musical subscenes during any particular time span. I'm thoroughly convinced that this methodology enabled my further research into the objects. Kate, on the other hand, just complained that I spent too much time "fondling" my records—and maybe there's some truth to that observation as well.

Without even realizing it, I was apparently taking the next natural step for a serious collector: with my index cards, I was creating a *catalog* of the collection's "holdings." On a conscious level, I was simply embarking on an effort to get a grip on the information embodied in the records. But on a deeper level, perhaps I was just acting out what Philipp Blom notes is a trait all collectors share: the need for "keeping track and asserting [our] control over the small corner of the world in which [our] will count[s] for something." Either way, my own ultimate feelings on all this cataloguing activity are perfectly reflected in Blom's thought that "without his catalogue, every major collector has to fear the dispersal of his collection and his own descent into obscurity. A catalogue is not an appendage to a large collection, it is its apogee." With no plans for dispersing my collection anytime soon, and with a realistic sense that an obscure collector was precisely what I was, I spent much more effort developing my collection itself rather than the catalog that documented it.

In fact, by this time in my collecting life I'd decided to become more serious about protecting my growing "archive" of materials in a manner consistent with professional standards. For years I'd been placing each record (45, 78, or LP) in individual, specially made, protective Mylar sleeves. But I was interested in what additional steps might be taken. This led me to read Jerry McWilliams's 1979 book, *The Preservation and Restoration of Sound Recordings*, from which I learned the latest archival techniques for the proper cleaning, playback, and storing of valuable records. This new commitment soon led me to discover and join a national organization of experts and institutions with a similar interest, the Association for Recorded Sound Collections (ARSC).

In time I began to attend annual conferences of the ARSC, and this deeper involvement with that organization ultimately resulted in my being asked to serve on their blue-ribbon committee for publishing excellence. This proved to be a fun crew that evaluated the very best recording-industry history books and essays published each year and determined which merited official recognition and awards. It was this new role that afforded me access to the minds of some of the nation's top experts on the history of recording—not to mention freebie copies of some really fine music research tomes. And it was through my interactions with professional archivists among the ARSC membership that the idea and value of a formal, institutional, recorded-sound archive began to take shape in my mind.

By 1983 I was jabbering about organizing a historical preservation effort that could be called the Northwest Music Archive (NWMA).

In these daydreams it was easy to think that down the road Seattle might have a museum-like repository that could serve as a public research base and a center for celebrating our history.

Like any zealot, I managed to ignore information that clashed with my vision—in this instance, there was always that lingering thought that perhaps not a single other individual would care as much about this slice of regional arts and industrial history as I did. I overcame these doubts by simply believing that through education and greater awareness the community would eventually embrace the idea warmly. And thus, the brainstorming went apace. As a vision for the NWMA formed, the outline of its mission and goals became clearer: "To preserve and document. To develop a publicly accessible computerized resource data-base. To initiate an educational activities program. And to acquire a permanent site to house and display historical artifacts."

Well, for an unemployed guy dwelling in a shabby apartment, I must at least be credited for thinking in ambitious terms! The thing is, a crazy idea can take off just as easily as a sane one—and the danger comes when others start taking your crazy ideas seriously. That's exactly what happened with the NWMA. I spread word of my plan around town with media friends and instantly got a bite: on February 26, 1983, I appeared as a guest for a radio special we called *The Archive Hour*, which was broadcast from the UW campus's alternative-music radio station, KCMU.

In between playing some of the rarest and coolest local records from the past six decades, I talked up the NWMA idea and was a bit surprised by the number of enthusiastically supportive phone calls. Encouraged, I decided to develop an exhibit titled 50 Years of Hit-Making in the Pacific Northwest, to gauge the community's level of interest. I organized a number of artifacts—photographs of the earliest local recording studios, the bands that used them, and the records that were issued by pioneering local labels—and I wrote some explanatory labels that tied the whole conglomeration into a coherent display.

I approached Neil Heiman (my former boss at Peaches Records), and he instantly agreed to let me mount the exhibit on the back wall of his huge store. The final display included examples of locally cut records ranging from the earliest Morrison label pressings up through a rare copy of the Kingsmen's "Louie Louie" (as originally and briefly issued on Seattle's Jerden Records label, before the song broke out nationally on the much larger New York–based Wand label). I also included a couple of autographed discs by the most recent rock band to have success in the town's studios, Heart.

I drew up a press release that asserted, "A greater awareness of our past—the legacy of early Northwest musical traditions—can foster a deeper appreciation within the community for current Northwest music. A continuum of respect is essential for the development of a healthy music scene as well as an expansive local industry." The media responded favorably with significant advance coverage, and when the exhibit opened in May 1983, I was pleasantly surprised at the local media's positive response

Seattle's top rock 'n' roll magazine, *The Rocket,* ran the headline "Northwest History on Display"; the *Seattle Post-Intelligencer's* Gene Stout called me for a brief interview and then touted the exhibit in his column, describing the show's content and reporting that "the Northwest Music Archive eventually hopes to find a permanent location for the collection and plans to expand it to include many more Northwest musicians. 'Most people are aware that Bing Crosby, Jimi Hendrix, and Heart had their beginnings in the Northwest,' [Blecha] said. 'But there are thousands of other great musicians who deserve recognition.'"

With these media assists, the exhibit saw a pretty good turnout and I enjoyed manning the gallery, answering questions, and accepting donations of artifacts from a few benefactors. Encouraged by the positive response, I pitched doing a regular column to *The*

Rocket's editors, a column based on all the history I was digging up. And so my Northwest Music Archive column launched in September, with a feature on Dave Lewis, the king of Seattle's 1950s R&B. The long-running NWMA column helped establish me as the local-music history guy.

The publicity from the exhibit also sparked a wave of invitations from a number of local radio stations. Over the next year I made appearances on KEZX, KING AM, KOMO, KASY, KQUL, KLSY, KSER, and KBCS. And each time I dragged along my little metal box full of rare 45s and evangelized about how cool local music really was. I also produced two *Northwest Music Archive Hour* shows at KCMU and even made a couple of TV appearances.

I became convinced that the original exhibit could be developed into a bigger attraction. With an expanded concept, additional arti-facts, new exhibit labels, and a new title—The History of Recording in the Northwest—it was ready. Aiming a bit higher, I pitched the idea to management at the downtown Seattle Public Library. By this point I already had such faith in the idea that I wasn't surprised when they promptly agreed and offered gallery space in their music section to mount the show.

This second, larger exhibit opened in November 1984, and once again the local media helped out—the *Seattle Weekly's* coverage was headlined "Sound Display," and Stout's *P-I* piece ("New Show Traces History of Recording in the Northwest") included more of my boilerplate blather that was starting to sound uncannily like a mission-statement-in-the-works: "The Northwest Music Archive is dedicated to the documentation and preservation of the Northwest's musical heritage."

WRITING HISTORY

In the late 1980s I reluctantly quit my job at Golden Oldies—an enjoyable gig at Seattle's ground zero for rare 45 singles, and thus a place where I met tons of area musicians (including young players who would later surface in famous grunge-era bands like Pearl Jam and Soundgarden). But I received a better offer from Park Avenue Records over in the Fremont neighborhood that, as they say, I just couldn't refuse. This firm was a combination used-record shop and active record label that had enjoyed considerable recent success issuing punk rock records by the Wipers and the Visible Targets. Working there was my chance to see "from the inside" how a small, independent rock label operated, and I took it.

The owner-operator, Bob Jeniker, was another interesting character. A Butte, Montana, native, he'd gotten involved in digging out collectibles way back in the late 1960s and was personally responsible for draining that state of probably half the records, jukeboxes, old electric guitars, and circa 1800s Tiffany leaded-glass windows it ever contained. Recently relocated to Seattle from Portland, he needed help sorting, pricing, and racking his tens of thousands of rare 78s and 45s. I was just the guy to pitch in, and when hired I felt I'd landed the ultimate job.

Because of that killer stock, and Jeniker's winning personality, over the years Park Avenue became a destination hotspot for many high-profile collectors, including eccentric customers that ranged from the famed cartoonist-illustrator R. Crumb to the Dead Kennedys' vocalist, Jello Biafra. The best thing of all was that Jeniker placed me in charge of his backroom mail-order operation, which was a very welcome change from manning a sales counter and dealing with hordes of maniacal record collectors!

But Jeniker and I also undertook expeditions together to look over, appraise, and/or buy a good number of very large record collections. From Jeniker (as well as from Golden Oldies' Dean Silverstone),

I learned a simple retail truth that every used-record shop knows: only an exceedingly small number of people have successfully sold off a big record collection profitably.

In almost every case imaginable, a collection's owner will always value that collection more highly than a retailer, who can't factor in the emotional significance it represents to the person who built it up over time. But with a straightforward and honest approach, a buyer is often able to work around the seller's inevitable disappointment and successfully acquire quite large record collections—some in the high hundreds or even thousands of units—with both parties adequately satisfied with the transaction.

Some of the biggest collections we bought required Jeniker and me to take a field trip together. Although usually these were target specific—in response to a collector's call—perhaps the most memorable road adventure was just the opposite. We decided one time to just jump in the van and go on a long drive, scouring thrift shops and record stores from Seattle all the way to Jeniker's hometown of Butte. Though it felt more like a vacation than work, there was plenty of labor involved—and *man* did we ever scoop up the goods! I fondly recall the two of us wrapping up long days of driving and hunting down discs by checking into cheap motels in hot places like Spokane, Lewiston, Missoula—and probably even Bumfuck, I don't remember now—showering up, getting dinner somewhere, spending the evening checking out country bands in local bars, and finally returning to our room, where we sat around well into the wee hours blissfully spinning all of that day's mystery disc finds on a crummy little 45 player we'd dragged along with us. Those were great times!

Later, Jeniker and I collaborated on a few reissue projects that helped revive interest in classic and obscure Northwest oldies. The first one we began pushing was a compilation album based on the recorded works of perhaps Seattle's hippest psychedelic-era folk-rock group, the Daily Flash. Jeniker was friends with a couple of the band members, and they really supported the idea of trying to get their material back into the marketplace—their recordings had been out of print for almost twenty-five years. Our goal was to compile the band's original four songs, which had been issued by two major labels back in 1965–67, with some real rarities: a previously unreleased studio session from a few unique acetate discs we'd turned up, and some live concert tracks that had been captured during the band's prime. While I researched and wrote liner notes (and Kate designed the cover), Jeniker handled the record production details, which finally culminated in December 1984 with the release of the *I Flash Daily* LP, issued by the British label Psycho Records.

We were all very pleased that our first project together had come to fruition. But there would be others as time went on. Jeniker happened to know the Santa Monica–based execs in America's most-active reissue-oriented record label, Rhino Records. So the following year, 1985, saw the release of *The Best of the Kingsmen*, for which I'd selected the songs and penned the liner notes.

On a roll, Jeniker and I proposed to Rhino that we produce a compilation album of classic Northwest gems. After much work securing proper licenses and audio sources for our chosen songs, Rhino released the LP *Nuggets Volume 8: The Northwest* in early 1987. Jeniker and I were very pleased that we'd pulled off what many fans had thought impossible: a compilation that (unlike the handful of other single-label-type releases) actually managed to present bands whose recordings were controlled by a number of different (and competitive) labels. It was gratifying to see the first review (by *Seattle Times* critic Patrick MacDonald), which praised the LP as "a particularly well-thought-out collection, from the wide-ranging selections to the excellent liner notes by Peter Blecha, the Northwest rock historian."

Henceforth, my reputation as a capable liner-note author snowballed and I would subsequently be hired to write for a string of additional Northwest compilations, including Etiquette Records' *Here Are the Ultimate Sonics* CD, England's Big Beat Records' *Psycho-Sonics*

CD, and the *NW Battle of the Bands* CD. In addition, Jerden Records hired me for several projects. I served as creative director (and wrote the notes) for what became the company's three-volume *History of Northwest Rock* CD series (*The Original Northwest Sound [1959–1964], The Garage Years [1963–1967],* and *Psychedelic Seattle [1965–1969]*). I did the same for their *Maintaining My Cool* Sonics CD and their (as-yet-unreleased) Dave Lewis Trio disc, *Deep Roots: The Best of Seattle's R&B King.*

Thus, all my years of archiving rare recordings, conducting oral histories with musicians, and compiling obscure information were being rewarded. I now had the opportunity to place the musical accomplishments of the Northwest's music industry in a historical context—and to help rescue some long-out-of-print vintage music, making it available to a potentially wider new audience.

► Nirvana's 1988 debut Sub Pop single: "Love Buzz"/"Big Cheese."

LOVE BU
b / w
BIG CHE

KURDT KO
VOCALS, GUIT
CHRIS NOVO
BASS
CHAD CHAN
DRUMS

RECORDED AT RECIPROC
SEATTLE. PRODUCED B
DINO & NIRVANA.

PHOTOGRAPHS BY ALI
INNER LABEL DESIGN BY S
JACKET DESIGN BY

LOVE BUZZ WRITTEN BY ROBBY VA

60 /1000

MUSEUM-WORTHY ARTIFACTS?

My Northwest Music Archive column in *The Rocket*—even more so than the many liner notes I was writing—caused a lot of people to take my work seriously, and some began donating items to the cause. Among these supporters was Seattle's top poster designer Art Chantry, who gave me hundreds of local rock posters. My friend Steve Ahlbom (the Debbies' singer, and a noted poster designer as well) likewise donated a similar amount—a stash that happened to include several of his own and Art Chantry's earliest and rarest posters from the late 1970s. Another musician pal, Dennis Caldirola, donated nearly fifty 1970s rock-band T-shirts. And Tom and Ellen Ogilvy (operators of the hit-making 1960s teen R&B label, Sea-fair-Bolo Records) generously gave a good number of 45s from their large catalog that were proving to be difficult to find elsewhere.

Finally, the Ogilvys' contemporary counterparts—friends who launched the first successful record companies to emerge from Seattle in two decades—actively supported my efforts by donating one of everything they produced. This meant items from Nastymix Records, the hip-hop label behind Sir Mix-A-Lot's rise as an international phenom; and from Sub Pop Records, which gained global fame with such grunge-era bands as Nirvana, Soundgarden, and Mudhoney.

Between the record-shop folks and label execs, more and more people were beginning to understand my goal of establishing a definitive archive that would represent the entire breadth of music, entertainment, and recording history from our region. Even though this may have seemed like an unrealistic undertaking then, I was committed to it, firmly believing that one day my collection would deserve to be housed in a serious museum of one form or another.

Although extremely busy, I was rather satisfied with what I considered to be serious progress in my chosen quest. But leave it to Kate to once again intervene with the big-picture truth: as she saw it, I was still muddling too much in the small time. She suggested that I return to the UW and finally secure a degree in something practical. I looked into it and decided that, yes, I could salvage all my past credits, take a series of additional classes, and come out with a degree in museum sciences, or museology.

In fall 1988 I signed up for college once again. I enjoyed the introductory museology classes immensely, scored an A, and decided to seek the advice of the head of the anthropology department. After interviewing me about my main interests—regional music history—he told me that my focus was already so specialized that I need not complete museology studies. Rather, he suggested I round out my education with some additional practical skills, like photography and typing. After all, he said, "some of history's finest museum professionals never got a degree." So, just that easily—and for the second time—I allowed myself to get talked out of continuing down the academic path.

But as I closed one door of opportunity, another magically swung open. That very same season I crossed paths with Bart Becker, a talented writer at the *Seattle Weekly*, and he took an interest in my Northwest music obsession. I invited him over to my place to tour the Northwest Music Archive, as I was now calling my collection, and to discuss my goals. One thing led to another, and when the December 28, 1988, issue of the *Weekly* hit the stands it included a lengthy profile titled "Seattle's Curator of Rock 'n' Roll—Peter Blecha Brushes the Dust out of the Grooves of Northwest Music History." The essay told of my research efforts, my long-term interest in collecting, and the current status of the collection.

In response to my daydreaming of a museum or some kind of institution to honor the accomplishments of local musicians, Becker in his article offered this sobering observation: "Still, concrete plans for a rock archives—a *place*, for example—are more problematic. Blecha's collection is hardly art in the Seattle Art Museum sense, nor the kind of dusty artifacts valued by academia. Come back in a couple hundred years and maybe we'll talk about it."

SHOW AND TELL

Any head shrinker can tell you that the supremely ironic flip-side of many a secretive collector's obsession for hunting, gathering, and then hoarding is the seemingly contradictory need to occasionally show the collection off to others. While there's plenty of pleasure to be had by enjoying our collections in private, part of the typical collector's psyche includes the internal urge to gain a sense of distinction by "sharing" their finds with the world.

This was undeniably one of the goals I developed in assembling my collection. With neither of the town's major institutions—the Seattle Art Museum (SAM) and the Museum of History and Industry (MOHAI)—showing interest in locally produced music or the history of our music industry, I felt something had to be done to try to break through the inertia of ignorance. And if I could carve out a job or career based on my growing knowledge, well, all the better.

It was some time after our marriage that Kate suggested I confront the matter head-on and explore whatever faint possibilities might exist. And so, in fall 1989 I cold-called the executive director of MOHAI, Carl Lind, and requested a meeting. A week later he welcomed me to his office, where we discussed a few ideas I had for developing a Northwest music exhibit at his museum. I presented him with a folder of press clippings about my previous independent exhibits, along with a description of the artifact holdings in the Northwest Music Archive, and thanked him for his time. Lind agreed to ponder it all, and I went on my merry way.

That same winter I accepted an invitation from KCMU and began hosting a weekly radio show that spotlighted interesting recordings from the Northwest. The station's news magazine, *WIRE*, promoted the show by stating, "Blecha has more than 15,000 recordings by Northwest artists in his collection that he will dip into each Tuesday evening." My archives were still growing. With no limitations on the musical content, it was an incredibly eclectic show, featuring a jumble of both impossibly obscure oldies (vintage lumberjack tunes, 1950s doo-wop rarities, honking R&B, Seattle's earliest punk 45s from the 1970s) and new singles by up-and-coming little bands with names like Nirvana, Mudhoney, and the Screaming Trees. My goal was to spark a greater awareness that our history was deeper than one might first suspect—and listener responses approved.

A couple months had raced by when I received a phone call from Bob Scheu, the operations manager at MOHAI. As I recall, he said he'd just been reviewing various submissions in an effort to identify potential museum volunteers and had come across the materials I'd left with his boss. Luckily, Scheu didn't ask me to volunteer as an usher in their auditorium or as a parking lot attendant, but instead said he thought a Northwest music exhibit had real potential. We met up and discussed the possibility, the extent of my collection, and the problems MOHAI had been facing in drawing crowds to its shows in recent years. I already knew that the museum had long suffered a reputation as a precious plaything of the dowdy blue-haired ladies who had founded it back in 1952. Though many Seattle natives fondly remembered the museum from grade-school field trips, it was decidedly *not* a cutting-edge institution, and it had been struggling to draw new audiences and attract the larger crowds that might bring its budget into the black.

I knew that a music-history exhibit was perfectly aligned with MOHAI's formal mission of presenting shows about local history and industry. And with portions of such a show highlighting the diverse cultural fields of rock 'n' roll, jazz, country, and R&B—including that famed hometown guitarist, Jimi Hendrix, and his youthful days on the scene—it might even attract an entirely new, young, and racially diverse audience. What was not to like?

So Scheu and I kicked ideas around and by May 1990, we submitted a proposal for the History of Northwest Rock and Roll exhibit—to be produced by MOHAI staff, guest curated by myself, and mounted in the January to June window that was still open in the museum's 1991 schedule. When in a second iteration of the proposal my formal role morphed into merely that of consultant, I was still thrilled. The main goal, after all, was to have this project take off, and the prospects of that were looking great. Though a music exhibit was an unusual idea for MOHAI, director Lind seemed game—with the caveat that we still had a few bureaucratic hurdles to jump.

First, MOHAI's board of directors needed to be persuaded. They asked that we demonstrate what level of developmental funding support might be available from the community. With the zeal of missionaries, we set out to persuade successful local entertainment-industry figures that an exhibit that would, in part, salute their forebears in the theater, radio, recording, and talent-booking biz would be a desirable thing. In no time, initial pledges (albeit ones dependent on matching funds) mounted toward our budget's six-figure goal. *That* really got the MOHAI bigwigs' attention.

The board, understandably, moved to form a committee to take a closer look at our concept. With these important hurdles being successfully navigated, it seemed as if we would soon have a thumbs-up from all relevant and necessary parties. But after all this dizzying and positive momentum, the wheels inexplicably began to turn much more slowly. The whole thing fell into a state of mysterious dead-time inertia. Although the exhibit was a seemingly great and eminently doable idea, month after month of delay finally added up to two years of waiting for a *formal* go-ahead and MOHAI's commitment to locked-in dates. Meanwhile, I stayed focused, busily organizing (and collecting more) artifacts, outlining potential exhibit storylines, and—admittedly jumping the gun a little—even roughing out some label-text samples.

In hindsight, the earliest hint of what was going on behind the scenes was Scheu's gingerly worded diplomatic olive branch in our initial proposal: "I hope I am not stepping on anyone's toes with this proposal. I am responding to an apparent need with the best idea we've had in a while." And in a follow-up memo a week later he added:

"P.S. I really appreciate everybody's willingness to continue to talk about this idea in spite of the source (left field?)." To be sure, it was very unusual for a museum's *building manager* to get involved in shepherding an exhibit idea through the system. But we felt the idea had enough positive attributes to ensure its survival against any legitimate challenges.

Still, by late 1991 I'd begun to wonder what the problem was. Trying to prompt some action, we put in another request for MOHAI to commit to the next available window of March to November 1992. No response came. In time, rumors finally suggested that members of the MOHAI Curatorial Department were feeling a little bit threatened by a "guest consultant" coming in and helping develop what could conceivably be one of the most successful exhibits the museum had ever mounted.

Meanwhile, during these very same years, Seattle's music scene had exploded on the world stage, and our grunge-rock phenomenon had made the Northwest the acknowledged center of the rock 'n' roll universe. I continued to systematically collect thousands of artifacts representing this history, a history that now suddenly had a stunning coda: the long-awaited triumph of Seattle's recording industry. But if MOHAI staff couldn't get over silly fears of sharing credit with a consultant, it was their missed opportunity—certainly not one that would make me abandon my interest in documenting the unfolding story of Northwest music history.

A BIG OL' PILE OF STUFF

By 1990 the Northwest Music Archive was an unrivaled collection whose bulk physically dominated Kate's and my Lake Union apartment. With this acute cramping as an impetus, we tried to get some grasp of the numerical size (and of the monetary value, for property-insurance purposes) by undertaking an inventory. We spent an hour every evening (all summer long) with me pawing through every item, one by one, and Kate writing notes as I called out two numbers for each item: the original cost (as best I could recall) and my appraisal of its current street value.

This tedious process finally resulted in some statistics that are worth sharing. Among the Northwest holdings were more than 6,500 singles; 1,600 LPs; 500 78s; 350 reel-to-reel, cassette, and 8-track tapes; 165 CDs; and 100 ultrarare acetates (including ones by Bonnie Guitar, the Brothers Four, the Kingsmen, the Sonics, the Bards, the Raymarks, the Bumps, the New Yorkers, the Squires, Ian Whitcomb, Mr. Lucky and the Gamblers, Springfield Rifle, Crome Syrcus, Washington Natural Gas, Danny O'Keefe, and the Screaming Trees). In addition, there were the print materials: more than 3,500 music magazines; 2,500 performance posters, handbills, and cards; 1,000 radio charts; 800 examples of vintage sheet music; 300 photographs; 75 concert programs (1904–1980s); 50 books; and 150 Hendrix LPs and 45s. Finally, we also counted 2,000-plus miscellaneous items like buttons, stickers, postcards, and other ephemera related to various local bands and labels.

The grand total was close to 20,000 items. But these numbers really don't reflect the true nature of how my initial interest in local music history had led to such a huge collection. I started out with local garage rock and Northwest teen R&B 45s from the 1960s. It was in searching for these items that I discovered the earlier, fantastic local 1950s rockabilly and doo-wop. And this was only the beginning: I ended up collecting numerous and sundry subcategories of Northwest music. Local musicians playing ragtime, Dixieland, gospel, swing, blues, bluegrass, country, square dance, folk, folk rock, soul, acid rock, funk, country rock, progressive rock, heavy metal, disco, punk, New Wave, grunge, and hip-hop. Amusing records representing the region's versions of 1960s girl groups and teen-idol types, twist-era combos, surfer rock, and British Invasion–wannabe bands. My completist urge also caused me to branch out from Washington music history to that of Oregon, Idaho, and Montana as well. If you can name it, rest assured, I collected it.

I collected entire categories that I'd once studiously ignored, like records cut by wimpy hotel orchestras and lounge bands, public school orchestras and choirs, church (and pizza parlor) pipe organists, sorority and fraternity glee clubs, and all those tortuous vanity records self-financed by scores of local amateur "songwriters" and "singers" who felt the need to share their "talents" with the rest of the world. I'd gathered up discs of locally made radio station (and other corporate) ad jingles, political campaign songs, comedy, ethnic music (Scandinavian accordion trios, Yakima Valley Mexican bands, Northwest Native American ceremonies), sports team anthems, and a stack of Seattle 1962 World's Fair–related records that almost rivaled the Space Needle in height.

Then there were the rare discs issued by local 1950s kiddie TV show hosts like Sheriff Tex Lewis, Stan Boreson, and Wunda Wunda. And there were the *many* songs that mentioned Seattle in their titles, like the old 78 of "Go See Seattle" by Ted Weems and His Orchestra, or Perry Como's and Bobby Sherman's competing versions of the *Here Come the Brides* TV show theme, "Seattle." Fifty-six compilation LPs were devoted to Northwest artists, and other more-provincial gems included the 1980 Mount St. Helens–theme records and plenty of novelty radio hits like "Bigfoot," "The Geoduck Song," "D. B. Cooper Where Are You?," "The Aroma of Tacoma," "Acres of Clams," "Boeing Boeing 707," and, of course, every known local rendition of the region's unofficial rock 'n' roll song, "Louie Louie." This collecting ultimately resulted in nearly complete runs of almost every label that had been founded here, from the earliest (Evergreen, Rainier, and Morrison) to the golden era of 1960s rock (Etiquette, Jerden, and Seafair-Bolo), right up through the town's two latest success stories (Nastymix and Sub Pop).

Among all this quantity were the region's crown jewels: a 78 of Jelly Roll Morton's 1919 boogie-woogie classic, "Seattle Hunch"; lots of Roaring Twenties major-label 78s featuring local dance bands like Vic Meyers and His Hotel Butler Orchestra, Jackie Souders and His Orchestra, and Cole McElroy's Spanish Ballroom Orchestra; the first locally recorded jazz 78, Norm Bobrow and the Gay Jones Trio's "Darktown Strutter's Ball" from 1945; a few 78s (circa 1945-46) from probably the first country band to see records issued by a local label, Cherokee Jack Henley and His Rhythm Ridin' Wranglers; the first R&B record ever cut in Seattle, young Ray Charles's 1948 debut, "Confession Blues"; the Northwest's earliest teenage African-American doo-wop recordings, those 1955–56 (*purple* vinyl!) 45s by Tacoma's Barons; Willie Nelson's ultrarare 45 cut in 1957 when he was a struggling radio DJ/singer in Vancouver, Washington; Loretta Lynn's rare debut single cut in 1960 when she lived in Custer, Washington; the 45 that probably deserves credit as the first locally recorded rock record, Joe Boot and the Fabulous Winds' "Rock and Roll Radio" from 1958; the Ventures' two hotly sought-after Blue Horizon label singles that were self-released prior to their break-out in 1960; a 45 cut by the teen band Thomas and His Tomcats, a mere two months after their guitarist (Jimi Hendrix) split to join the army in 1961; the Kingsmen's ultrarare picture-sleeve-clad potato-chip ad jingle 45, "The Krunch"; Sonics records made in Spain and France (and even a few bootlegs!); and a disc that's been hailed as one of the "top five collectible LPs in the world," the 1968 self-titled psychedelic masterpiece by Portland's New Tweedy Brothers, replete with its uniquely octagonal, silver-metallic mirror-finish cardboard jacket; and on and on . . .

Collecting vintage dance and concert posters was one of my favorite activities—and I think I've proved that I have a particular knack for sniffing out the goods. Among my thousands were posters promoting a 1923 dance at the Mount Vernon Armory; a 1930s "All Night Dance" at the Richmond Beach Pavilion; an early 1950s

New Year's Eve dance with Sheriff Tex and His Jamboree Gang; Bill Haley and His Comets' 1956 and 1957 Evergreen Ballroom shows; and various early rockabilly shows at the legendary Spanish Castle Ballroom. Over time I had even dug up awesome posters for early rock bands including the Wailers, the Teen Kings, the Ventures, the Kingsmen, the Dynamics, the Sonics, the Bootmen, Paul Revere and the Raiders, Merrilee Rush and the Turnabouts, and Don and the Goodtimes.

Then there were many examples of those now highly prized Fillmore-style psychedelic era posters for Northwest bands like the Daily Flash, the Magic Fern, Floating Bridge, Crome Syrcus, Easy Chair, and the Initial Shock; and for the area's hippie happenings like the Trips Festival, Seattle Potlatch, and the Sky River Rock Festival. Other posters evoked the 1970s club scene, which produced top bands like Heart, Big Horn, Gabriel, and Thin Red Line. That same decade eventually brought the dada-influenced graphic nihilism of the punk movement, represented by new regional bands such as the Enemy, the Wipers, the Lewd, D.O.A., and the Subhumans. Finally, there were tons of posters that marked the rise of Seattle's grunge bands: Nirvana, Soundgarden, Pearl Jam, Alice in Chains, Pond, Sunny Day Real Estate, and the Screaming Trees.

In terms of magazines, all told I'd gathered more than two hundred different publications that featured (or at least contained some) music-scene coverage. Among them were the mid-1960s *KJR Beat* and *Disc-A-Go-Go*; a number of 1960s underground/hippie papers like the *Avatar, Sabot, Puget Sound Partisan*, and a nearly complete run of Seattle's very first, the *Helix*. Then came the 1970s to 1980s punk scene, and with it, early rags like *Chatterbox, Seattle Buzz, Stellazine, Desperate Times, The Rocket, Attack, Answer Me!, Bored, The Underground, Street Kids, Face It, Curse*, and *Hype*.

All in all, I figured that I had accumulated materials that documented the activities of more than 5,000 different recording acts. So, whether in collaboration with the crew over at MOHAI or not, I remained committed to finding a way to take the next step and see that my collection found a proper home—that is, somewhere other than *my own* (the modest little house in Seattle's Ravenna area that Kate and I bought in 1991). Anyone who has seen the interior of a house inhabited by a serious collector knows what I mean. Whether they live in an apartment, condo, or house, collectors tend to gather more and more of their prized things until their own living space is severely compromised.

I know about this firsthand because these couple decades of active collecting resulted in what can only be described as a "full house." That Kate ever indulged me to the extent that massive record and poster collections were stored on racks along the walls of our bedroom still amazes me. The only reason they were stacked in there, though, was because the larger bulk of them had already filled our entire basement, with the exception of a tight space reserved for our washer, dryer, water heater, and furnace. The guest room that Kate and I had envisioned? Consumed by my collection. The music room? Well, the drums, guitars, amps, and piano were definitely in there, but because it was crammed with records, accommodating jam sessions with musician pals wasn't feasible. Even my latter-day dream of having a hobby-rock weekend band was being affected by the mounding archives.

A breakthrough came when Kate finally suggested that we move to a larger home. I realized we had hit the critical point that comedian George Carlin had joked about in his 1981 routine "A Place for My Stuff." Riffing on the main purpose of houses, he'd said, "That's all you need in life: a little place for your stuff. You know? . . . That's *all* your house is. A *place* to keep your *stuff*. If you didn't have so much stuff, you wouldn't *need* a house. You could just walk around all the time. A house is just a pile of stuff with a cover on it . . . That's what your house *is*: a place to keep your stuff while you go out and get *more* stuff! Sometimes you gotta move—get a *bigger* house. *Why?* No room for your stuff anymore."

Truer words were never spoken, and Kate and I up and moved to a considerably larger, finer house. With our limited budget, how could we afford such a place? Tired of the spatial impediments my enormous archive was creating in our daily lives, I, to the shock of all who knew me, did the unthinkable: I sold my collection.

Manufac

▶ The Jimi Hendrix Experience's psychedelic 1967 single, "Purple Haze."

04

Deutsche Grammophon, Hamburg. Printed in Germany by Ludwig Fr. Noltemeyer, Braunschweig

59 072

HENDRIX EXPERIENCE

URPLE HAZE

THE JIMI HENDRIX MUSEUM

ow I came to sell my beloved collection is entangled within the saga of helping create a memorial to 1960s rock 'n' roll guitar god, Jimi Hendrix. The City of Seattle has always had a sketchy relationship with the legacy of its most famous native son, so while his fans had been clamoring for years for the city to make some significant gesture toward the musician's memory, the powers that be—apparently turned off by his iconic status as the psychedelic 1960s shaman *nonpareil*—had effectively brushed off any and all overtures.

The first grassroots effort to do positive things in his name dates back to 1971, when an extremely hazy nonprofit organization, the Jimi Hendrix Foundation, was launched. Born under a bad sign, the hastily organized group—which had somehow suckered in Jimi's father, Al Hendrix—died under a dark cloud of scandal without accomplishing its lofty goals. Then, a decade later, people began petitioning to get a street or a little park—*something*—renamed for Hendrix. That's when one group of fans hooked up with a local radio station to raise funds, in a well-intentioned effort to honor the late musician with some sort of public monument. The publicity this organization generated finally forced the city into talks.

Unfortunately, in the wake of negotiations with an unsympathetic bureaucracy, that monument took a regrettable form. To this day, you can visit the result at the rudest location possible: in the Woodland Park Zoo's African Savanna exhibit, a large chunk of *African* stone bears a brass plaque inscribed with a few words for Jimi and a big logo of the radio station. In my opinion, this is a civic embarrassment of the first order.

And that's where this frustrating situation stood for years. Until, that is, a shred of hope emerged in the form of an amazing little news item that appeared in the Seattle papers in 1992. Paul Allen, cofounder (with Bill Gates) of Microsoft and now a philanthropist, had announced his interest in *perhaps* establishing a gallery in Seattle to honor Jimi Hendrix, his musical hero. The article revealed that on September 3, an initial proposal had been proffered to a Seattle City Council committee for review. To the legions of Hendrix fans (myself included), this was all good news. With a powerful fan like Allen—also a skilled electric guitarist in his own right—there was hope once again that Jimi might finally get some formal respect in Seattle.

The story became more exciting when Bob Scheu from MOHAI called and filled me in on what he knew. It seemed that his earlier submission of a funding request for our planned Northwest music exhibit to Allen's main business-management company, Vulcan Northwest, had actually generated a response. But rather than offering to contribute to our MOHAI endeavor, Vulcan had invited Scheu to advise them on Allen's Hendrix gallery project. As that idea had stealthily moved forward, Scheu was asked to assemble a team of experts to contribute initial advice as consultants. This would be easy, as Scheu could essentially just revamp the original exhibit proposal for our now apparently aborted MOHAI show. In short, Scheu's Hendrix project proposal would list approximately the same team of specialists that had mainly been drawn from the ranks of his fellow employees at MOHAI.

A month flew by with only rumor-mill rumblings that Allen was thinking about locating the Hendrix exhibit in a small storefront downtown. As with all earlier proposals to locally honor Hendrix, the gallery idea brought out all the usual Hendrix haters—mainly a few grumpy folks who penned letters to the editors of the *Seattle Times* and *Seattle P-I* registering their displeasure that someone might be foisting a memorial to a "disgraceful and useless drug addict" on the people of Seattle.

I tried to counter these close-minded opponents by writing to the director of the Seattle Center, Virginia Anderson, voicing my support. In doing so, I wasn't shy about jumping ahead of the game a bit and asserting that "a museum founded in Jimi Hendrix's name seems *most* appropriate. Hendrix spent eighteen formative years in Seattle soaking up a lot of the local '50s jazz, rhythm-and-blues, and rock 'n' roll sounds of the Central District. A regional music museum would be an ideal opportunity for the greater community to have a chance to focus on, and be further educated about, our indigenous music forms and their historical development." The fact that Allen was only talking about a Hendrix exhibit, and *not* a "regional music museum," didn't slow me down one bit.

Meanwhile, behind the scenes—or at least under my radar—things were moving along at a rapid clip. Allen had designated his sister, Jody Allen Patton, to manage the development of the project, and I was soon invited (along with the MOHAI gang) to participate in an introductory kick-off meeting on October 1, 1992. I figured this was my big chance to push forward my dreams of a museum.

After introductions were made, Allen shared his vision for the project, which initially amounted to creating a vibrant home for the display of artifacts to honor Hendrix. Although the local media kept referring to the overall concept as relatively "modest" in the earliest coverage of the project, in fact the artifacts Allen had already acquired were *anything* but.

As a Hendrix memorabilia collector, I was accustomed to experiencing the minor thrill each time some new bootleg LP or old black-light head-shop poster turned up. But when Allen did a show-and-tell session with us, we were suddenly in the presence of iconic artifacts: the actual white 1968 Fender Stratocaster guitar that Jimi had famously played at the Woodstock Music and Arts Fair in 1969 (and that in 1990 had sold at a highly publicized Sotheby's auction for a record-setting sum of $320,000); the guitarist's Jax Vibra-Chorus distortion pedal device; and the black felt hat that Hendrix prominently wore on the *Smash Hits* LP cover.

Impressed with the extremely high quality of Allen's collection—not to mention his vision for the memorial gallery—we began our brainstorming. We were encouraged to dream aloud and told that

any and all ideas were good, that there were no barriers or limitations to the discussion. Everyone present was invited to kick in our
best ideas about what form such a new gallery might take. We were
asked to conjure up mental images of everything this new institution might be able to achieve, what it might contribute to the artistic
legacy of Jimi Hendrix, and what lasting value it might add to the
community.

Over a series of such sky's-the-limit meetings, talk soon turned
to potential gallery content—that is, what types of exhibits were even
possible and what kinds of artifacts would still be acquirable. Most
importantly, what "messages" would we want to convey through displays? Everyone at the table contributed exciting ideas, usually ones
that reflected their various areas of expertise. As a student of Hendrix's
history, and a collector of his music, my ideas were typically based
on a desire to get beyond the obvious biographical highlights of his
superstar glory years and to dig a bit deeper into his musical roots.

It seemed that this gallery represented a profound opportunity
to use this one artist's life story as a means of mining many other
rich veins of history. "Imagine display segments about Jimi's musical roots in the Northwest . . . the radio stations he'd been inspired
by, and the music he was exposed to early on . . . the local 'Louie
Louie'–era bands he had been a fan of . . . his own first three teenage
R&B bands . . . Jimi's subsequent chitlin' circuit road-tour days . . .
his Greenwich Village folk/blues-scene days . . . his arrival in London in late 1966 and the resultant fame that move brought," I told
the group.

For weeks the team met and energetically collaborated on countless exhibit themes, messages, and scenarios. Discussions ensued
about how we could take this further and also explore how Jimi's
story could be used to offer visitors insights into some of the musical
genres he'd been associated with, including blues, R&B, psychedelic acid rock, and funk. Maybe there could be some focus on the
communal celebration aspect of the 1960s rock festivals, like 1967's

Monterey Pop and 1969's Woodstock? Then again, maybe the exhibits could trace the musical predecessors who'd influenced Jimi—and, for balance, also trace Jimi's influence on subsequent generations of his musical progeny? All these attractive possibilities were exciting, and so was the leadership's response. As I later recalled this creative process to a reporter with *Vintage Guitar*, even early on "we were already saying, 'Look, this is not just "Purple Haze." We can tell a great story of *music* here.' They said, 'Great! Think bigger. What *else* could it be?'"

And so, with those heady marching orders, the team jammed on. Maybe the options being raised seemed infinite. I do believe that over time we explored, analyzed, and dissected pretty much every exhibit concept that held any real hope of being actualized—and plenty that didn't!

Along the way the gallery idea magically transformed into a far grander concept: the Jimi Hendrix Museum project. The growing sense that we had all jumped aboard a fast-moving roller coaster was enhanced by the Seattle City Council's unanimous decision, on October 19, to accept Allen's offer to build a museum at zero cost to the city or its taxpayers. By the following month the project would be stating publicly that the thing might open as soon as the summer of 1994. Then the first hard statistics—those defining a 10,000-square-foot space to be developed on a $400,000 budget—started showing up in the newspapers.

It was certainly exciting to see published proof of this dream-come-true in printed form. And better than that, it seems that I had contributed quite adequately to these early brainstorming sessions: a couple weeks later I was informed that Vulcan wished to use my services as a freelance archivist for their core planning team. This once-in-a-lifetime, gettin'-in-on-the-ground-floor deal was moving forward *and I was on board*.

Among the first tasks I took on at Vulcan was to initiate a clipping file, er, Institutional Archive that would document every media mention of our activities. Before long the team began to hammer out institutional mission and goals statements that would guide our thinking as we developed further philosophies, policies, and procedures. Eventually we discussed a few topics of keen interest to me: the project's collections development and exhibit development goals—goals that would be affected by the projected grand opening date. With a mere eighteen months of ramp-up time then facing us, it would require a Herculean effort to pull together enough quality artifacts and still have time to design them into displays, which themselves would then have to be installed.

So we fast-tracked planning about basics like what types of artifacts we wanted. Years later the museum's newsletter, *Feedback*, published a feature article titled "How to Build a World-Class Collection from Scratch," which asked, "And where do curators begin?" My response was, "In the beginning, there has to be consensus on what sorts of categories of artifacts would be interesting and crucial to have in the museum." Once the categories are determined, we would still face the issue of what kinds of individual artifacts would possibly qualify for consideration as an addition to the archives: "In short, there has to be a story behind each piece. 'It can't just be a rock curiosity—it has to go back to the story-telling imperative'" of our exhibit goals. In a different feature I also told *Feedback* that "overall, the idea is to collect objects that are interesting, but also have informational value, historical significance, and aesthetic appeal."

Toward that end—and once collecting for the Hendrix exhibit actually began—I would always try to determine which available artifacts held the most value for our exhibition purposes. This analysis was based on the significance of the history the item represented; on the potential for us to locate associated supporting materials (like films or photographs of the item in use); on the quality and condition of the item; and on how reasonable a seller's asking price was.

Meanwhile, Scheu—by now the project coordinator—had become entangled in conversations with a wily Hendrix collector whom I'd been aware of for years as a mail-order customer of ours back at Park Avenue. In January 1993, Scheu and I were sent out to the Midwest to look over a massive twelve-hundred-piece collection of Hendrix materials. This stash was one of the two or three best such Hendrix-centric collections in the world. In particular, it represented an unsurpassed amassing of every known Hendrix LP, EP, 45, and CD ever issued in any country around the globe (including Israel, Russia, Chile, Taiwan, France, Germany, Spain, Singapore, and England), along with what was recognized among fellow collectors as the world's finest assemblage of magazines featuring Hendrix's image on the cover.

I set about doing a review/appraisal of the items, looking to see that all the major rarities were accounted for and spot-checking random items for condition. Satisfied that the collection was as it had been described, we returned home with a report that went upstairs with Scheu's recommendation to go ahead—despite my reservations (the considerable asking price had, I think, clashed with my personal background as a low-end bargain picker and/or a retailer who had been trained to buy at wholesale). After discussions, a purchase of the collection was approved.

Once the items arrived here safely, we were all able to relax a bit, knowing that we could always rely on this massive archive of flashy artifacts to augment whatever particular exhibit might be mounted. In order to protect these and the other Hendrix artifacts, we arranged for storage space at a commercial high-security vault. With that step complete, it really began to seem like an actual museum was under way.

By February 1993, the team—which now consisted of Jody Patton, her assistant Sonia Heiman, Bob Scheu, a UW-based musicology grad student named Jim Fricke, myself, and three staffers from Seattle's esteemed Olson/Sundberg architectural firm, Walter Schacht, Dan Caine, and Zoe Melendez-Friedman—had begun going on information-gathering field trips to local institutions like the

Pacific Science Center, the Seattle Art Museum, and the Tacoma Art Museum. These initial visits allowed us to take "back of house" tours and pick the brains of top staffers, who happily advised us about topics ranging from specifics—like collections storage issues ("Get more than you'll ever think you'd need. Collections grow fast.")—to general dos and don'ts for avoiding pitfalls common to launching a new museum. These interactions were so informative that in March we took a five-day trip to Los Angeles with an itinerary that included the Museum of Contemporary Art, the Gene Autry Western Heritage Museum, Universal Studios, Disney's corporate offices, the Richard M. Nixon Library, and the Simon Wiesenthal Center's Museum of Tolerance.

As we progressed, the team's consciousness of what huge challenges we faced expanded—as did the ever-growing collection of Hendrix artifacts and the physical statistics for the museum. It wasn't too long before the *Seattle Times* ferreted out a few details, reporting that the project now had in mind a "15,000-square-foot, $400,000 exhibit earmarked for a small Seattle Art Museum building next to the Coliseum." That building was an underused SAM annex, the Seattle Art Pavilion, a box mainly recalled today as the site of the summer of 1978's blockbuster Treasures of Tutankhamun show.

By the fall of 1993, the team had come to realize that a main part of my expertise lay in artifact evaluation and authentication, and come November I was hired as a full-time archivist. I said farewell to my old job and friends at Park Avenue Records and gleefully stepped up to this major new opportunity.

In pondering the realistic lay of the land, it was apparent to me that to effectively mount the world-class Hendrix exhibits we were all dreaming about, we would need an incredibly rich archive of artifacts to select from. And recognizing that the museum's projected grand opening in the following summer would be sneaking up on us all too fast, there was no time for sitting around. The stated goal of building a definitive Hendrix collection could be accomplished only if we adopted a more aggressive approach to acquiring artifacts. Paul and Jody had similar feelings. We devised a system that involved filling out a recommendation form and submitting it with a presentation pitch whenever desirable artifacts surfaced in the marketplace. I quickly discovered that with an informed and rational explanation of an artifact's value to our exhibit goals, permission to proceed would likely be granted.

After some months—and a few hundred successful acquisition transactions—I was eventually promoted to curator of collections and granted the ability to, without prior approval, acquire appropriate items for the collection. Talk about your dream job!

Imagine the thrill of being able to reel in thousands of pricey artifacts—with someone else's money! Well, once I had that authority, I went at it with gusto. As the *Seattle Times* later put it, my "initial mandate was 'to scour the planet for world-class Hendrix artifacts, the crown jewels, the iconic pieces.'" I ramped up the museum's efforts to madly haul in anything interesting from the world of Hendrixiana. We acquired material that ranged from the sublime to the ridiculous, such as Hendrix's Octavio (prototype) distortion pedal, his King wah-wah pedal, stage apparel (including scarves, coats, pants, and a *second* black hat), several unique Hendrix acetate discs, a complete set (built over time) of genuine Hendrix gold (or platinum) record awards, the original artwork for the *Are You Experienced?* album, the original artwork for the Band of Gypsys' Fillmore East concert poster, two photographs of Hendrix performing in 1962 with the King Kasuals, eight photographs (with negatives) of Hendrix performing (and recording) with the Isley Brothers in 1964, copies of numerous ultrarare concert posters, vintage black-light head-shop posters, Mexican black velvet paintings, Hendrix memorial coins, an Asian Jimi doll squeeze toy, a set of Russian Hendrix nesting dolls, a Hendrix snowboard, a rare Hendrix Ice Cream Bar trading card, Hendrix refrigerator magnets, and perhaps the sickest of all—considering that they were actually marketed by the Hendrix estate itself—a Hendrix Christmas tree ornament, a Hendrix golf towel, and, believe it or not, bottles of red Jimi Hendrix–brand wine (one of the substances that had been cited as a factor in his death)!

All this time I kept a lookout for Hendrix records not yet in the collection. This process was a particular joy because I made it a priority to chase down what had long eluded my own collecting efforts—a few ultrarare 45s that represented Hendrix's earliest forays in recording studios. These were discs that other Hendrixologists had determined contained pre-fame guitar work by Jimi—most notably the otherwise obscure Los Angeles–based soul singer Rosa Lee Brooks's nearly priceless 1964 Revis Records single, "My Diary"/ "Utee." As I was able to check them off the want list, I felt a real sense of accomplishment. By the time the Hendrix Museum opened, I felt confident that it would indeed have the world's finest collection of such rarities.

Many such items were rustled up through the systematic scouring of dealers' ads in collectible record magazines like *DISCoveries*, *Record Collector*, and *Goldmine*. Others were acquired the old-fashioned way: by relentlessly monitoring the wares offered at record stores, collectors conventions, and junk shops. But perhaps the most enjoyable means was relying on serendipity to intervene—as it often did—in the form of the telephone on my desk ringing. It seemed that each day brought new surprises, some that were welcome, others not.

There had already been enough giddy media coverage of this museum-in-the-making that my phone was ringing off the hook with people wanting to donate or sell some artifact or another. I'd also quietly put the word out to many collectors and dealers around the world. The subtext of my message to these potential sources was that we might be interested in just about any quality Hendrix item, but that as an experienced collector I would expect to see sales offers come in with fair prices attached; just because a billionaire was entering the market didn't mean we would be throwing money around. And, it must be said, while a great number of sellers went on to conduct a healthy amount of business with us over the next years, there were a few who greedily tried to jack up prices on me, and I no longer responded to their calls.

More than a few callers, on the other hand, had the best of intentions and a spirit of generosity toward the project. A quite memorable fellow called in from Spokane to talk about an interesting item he had. With not a little chagrin after learning that I wanted to hear more about its provenance, he explained that as a young man he'd attended Hendrix's September 8, 1968, concert at the Spokane Coliseum. Because his father was a local cop he'd been able to watch the show from the backstage area. From that vantage point he was also in just the right place when, at the show's end, another audience member rushed onstage, grabbed Hendrix's wah-wah pedal, and made a mad dash for an exit door. As this caller explained, it was he who gave chase and helped corner the thief, and as I recall the telling, Hendrix's road crew was so grateful for the effort that he was allowed to keep the device. Now, almost three decades later, he wanted to donate the item to the museum, and after several subsequent conversations, during which I grilled him every which way in attempts to blow holes in his story, I was convinced of his honesty and happily honored his wish.

Other donors, though well meaning, just didn't know what they were talking about. For example, there was a donation that arrived on the museum's doorstep without a background story, documentation, or even any real leads as to its provenance. All we had was a claim that it was one of Jimi's trademark hippie blouses. Well, who knows? Now that it was here, the least we could do was have a look and see if some photographic or other kind of research was merited. One glance, however, was all that was required—the item was simply *not* as described. Rather than possibly being one of Hendrix's pieces of apparel, the thing was clearly a woman's dress.

One of our best, and most exciting, sources for acquiring serious artifacts was through competitive bidding at public auctions, including those held by houses such as Sotheby's, Christie's, Bonham's, and others. There was nothing more fun than receiving a new quarterly catalog and identifying items of potential interest, reviewing the listed opening bid figures (and the auction house's estimated sales price), conducting a bit of research as to marketplace values achieved for comparable items at previous auctions, and then the tricky part: determining a top spending limit for our bidding. That number is something we hashed out collectively, and the tactic generally worked out, but truth be told, on more than one occasion, it didn't, and we failed to win our targeted artifact.

The first auction I participated in was in San Francisco. The plan was to attend the preview (in a low-key, anonymous fashion), to study the items of interest that had been shown in a catalog, and then show up later that night to possibly bid during the actual live auction event. The items that seemed most attractive were a couple rare, vintage concert posters, and a typically flamboyant and psychedelic coat of many colors that Hendrix had once owned. Upon review, the artifacts measured up, and bidding at the auction hall proved successful for the museum.

But, what I didn't like one bit was the very public aspect of sitting among many other bidders and watching their eyes grow bigger with each sale. I also didn't appreciate that the managers of the auction house were now able to figure out who was representing Paul Allen's acquisition efforts. I had long been a firm believer in the value of having as much anonymity as possible while on the hunt for goodies. Yes, a collector needs to have friendly relations with sellers, and such connections can even be beneficial under certain circumstances; but allowing the auction crowd (and other Hendrix bidders in particular) to be able to associate a face—mine—with an aggressive collecting campaign didn't seem to be a good thing.

And so, that was the very last public auction I ever attended in person. From then on, whether it was an auction in Los Angeles, New York, or London, all the bidding was done by telephone. This of course meant that many a night's sleep over the next few years would be interrupted by a clanging alarm-clock waking me to get on the horn and sit there placing long-distant bids in the wee small hours.

THE INCREDIBLE
EXPANDING MUSEUM

The collections development process moved steadily forward—and in more directions than one. For one thing, the team's brainstorming had led to a tentative acceptance that the museum would probably benefit from having displays beyond those solely focusing on Hendrix. As the menu of wonderful ideas grew, I took every opportunity to evangelize about how Jimi provided us with a natural link—should we so wish—to develop additional exhibits about the broader story of Northwest music history. For example: not only had young Hendrix jammed with such early top local R&B bands as the Dave Lewis Combo, the Playboys, and the Sharps, but his direct influence on the guitar sounds employed by Seattle's current crop of so-called grunge rock bands—especially Pearl Jam—was undeniable.

Indeed, while collecting Hendrix stuff for the museum, I had also (on my own time) maintained a devoted interest in the ongoing evolution of the current local rock scene. That interest had included both going out regularly to see these grunge bands—the ones the world was venerating as the greatest thing in all rockdom—as well as collecting everything related to their rise. I had been tracking, collecting, and documenting some of these bands—or their precursor bands—since they'd first emerged around 1985, and I felt as much joy as probably anyone when Mudhoney, Soundgarden, the Screaming Trees, and Nirvana finally broke out and made such a phenomenal splash on the international stage.

But, truth be told, with all their (and other bands') activity and the resultant production of recordings (and artifacts related to that and touring), my ability to keep up was being sorely tested. This collecting was taking a severe toll on my pocketbook and was also adding serious bulk to the archives at home.

So it came as a great relief—both personal and professional—when the museum leadership one day took a decisive stand to broaden the institutional collecting from just Hendrix artifacts to Pacific Northwest music items. With that momentous change I instantly felt relieved of the self-imposed commitment to collect Northwest artifacts on my own dime. Just as I had earlier quit buying Hendrix items for myself—so as to avoid any conflict of interest with my employer—I was now able to stop adding to *my* Northwest collection and instead could steer everything that popped up straight into the museum project's vaults.

Interestingly, one important area of collecting didn't even require the direct expenditure of funds to actualize: current local performance posters. Given their ephemeral nature—it seemed as if a hundred different posters were distributed to record shops each week—it was obvious that to build a definitive collection we would need to engage the community's support. So I headed out to visit all the shopkeepers who had worked with me over the years and explained the new situation: I was no longer collecting personally, but if they'd like to continue helping, the museum project would appreciate it and we'd also be happy to purchase *any* and *all* good local records and CDs that turned up from now on.

My long-standing network of suppliers shifted over to the new plan; every week or two I'd make the rounds and these dealers really got into the spirit of things, pulling out stacks of freebie posters they'd held aside and then making good sales on whatever other items they'd found for me. The result was that for the next number of years we were the happy recipient of many thousands of such posters—all donated freely.

It sure didn't take long for word of the museum's new area of interest to spread among collectors, and I began swooping in to cut bulk deals for numerous locally based poster collections that ranged from hundreds of individual pieces on up. Perhaps the most memorable such deal was when I responded to one fellow's entreaty that I visit his Capitol Hill home for a look at his poster collection. He'd explained that the two thousand posters he was thinking of selling were those he'd gathered over twenty-plus years of regularly roaming up and down neighborhood streets and stopping by various record shops where posters always seemed to be stacking up in the freebie piles. That technique certainly rang a bell, and I assured him that I understood and would gladly come by to look and discuss.

When considering anything for the museum project's archives, I always felt the need to assess various factors, the foremost being quality and condition. The fact is the museum didn't need *everything*—it primarily needed historically significant or visually interesting pieces for display; any others would at best serve as archival items that could be of value to future researchers. But at the right price and in a favorable deal, quantity (and even duplicate spares) was not the enemy. Especially with a guy like this poster collector, who claimed to want to sell "all or nothin'."

I was truly shocked, though, when I arrived at his doorstep and beheld all two thousand posters—each assiduously stapled (four or more apiece) to all four walls *and* the ceiling of his entire house. At first glance I spotted many rare and desirable posters scattered among them, but it boggled the mind to ponder the neck-straining labor it would take to climb up and down a ladder, removing each and every one individually, not to mention that I couldn't determine the condition of the better ones prior to their suffering the inevitable damage that would result from a staple puller tool or, God forbid, a butter knife or some such improper implement.

I explained to the hopeful would-be seller that if he was willing to gamble the time required to yank them all down and place them in stacks—*and* if I was then happy with the condition that they were in—it was conceivable that we could cut a deal. He spent many days at the task and the house was stripped bare of all its decor. I returned to face mound after mound of posters, and the marathon task of appraising their combined value began in earnest. Fortunately, as I was only partway into the job, he made things very easy by blurting out what sales figure he'd had in mind. As it compared quite favorably with where my numbers were headed, I stopped right there, cut the deal, and we were both happy lads.

Beyond low-budget rock posters grabbed from record shops or torn down from telephone poles, there was another stratum of posters produced in the 1990s. In fact, the era represented a veritable renaissance of poster design, with now-famous designers like Mark Arminsky, Charles Burns, Art Chantry, Coop, Ellen Forney, Ed Fotheringham, Justin Hampton, Jeff Kleinsmith, Frank Kozik, and Joe Newton leading the way. These artists breathed new life into an old art form by reviving widespread appreciation for bold and beautiful posters of a quality unseen since the masterworks produced by Rick Griffin, Alton Kelley, Victor Moscoso, Stanley Mouse, and Wes Wilson in San Francisco's psychedelic heyday in the 1960s.

However, these high-quality, often limited-edition, signed and numbered, and usually silk-screened posters were *not* freebies. They were being sold to a new generation of collectors all over the world from out of fine shops like Seattle's Innervisions and Vox Populi, New York's Psychedelic Solutions, and Los Angeles's L'Imagerie. So acquiring these posters—the ones that promoted the top grunge bands from the Northwest—through purchase became another task in my growing portfolio of duties. Whenever possible, I visited the many galleries, buying interesting items in person. But on far more frequent occasions the deed was done by telephone after reviewing new sales catalogs that were periodically mailed out. By this point my museum-issued credit card was well used, and it certainly streamlined the acquisition process.

Lastly, one other early important area of building an archive for the museum had to do with music magazines. In addition to starting a research library by subscribing to just about every quality periodical known, I began systematically scouring retail racks at Barnes and Noble, Borders, and Tower Books—ultimately acquiring many hundreds of publications that contained cover articles or significant features about all the star grunge bands from the Northwest. What we might ever actually *do* with any of them I had no idea, but whether they might one day be displayed in a gallery or just used for research purposes, it seemed important to gather them here and now—before they went out of print and joined the burgeoning ranks of items considered rare and collectible.

Just as the collections for the Jimi Hendrix Museum had exploded in size, so too had other aspects of it. Though the tale of how all the changes occurred is a long and convoluted one probably best told elsewhere, I'll just mention that as the staff grew, and the number of excellent ideas continued to pour forth, the grand-opening date was repeatedly delayed—and this was good, as we all needed the extra time.

Under Paul and Jody's vision and leadership the team had finally settled on a couple key concepts that would be embodied in the institution's mission and goal statements, and would thus guide our subsequent developmental efforts. The museum would exist to explore *"creativity* and *innovation* as exemplified by popular music and culture." This idea seemed to be a rather brilliant construct on which to base the museum. It not only perfectly focused on Hendrix's main contributions to art, but also left things fairly wide open regarding what other subjects the team might eventually select for exhibits and other public programming.

All the churning of ideas the team engaged in while debating exhibit topics had resulted in a general consensus that there would never be a shortage of attractive possibilities. And thus, I for one was not at all disappointed when in early 1995 the museum called a press conference to announce a few major updates. We'd changed our name to the Experience Music Project (EMP), and we'd finally secured an official site (at Fifth Avenue and Denny Way, right below the Space Needle), where we would construct a big new building with an estimated interior size of 100,000 square feet and a budget of $50–$60 million.

These decisions were made only after some outside developments. After some misunderstandings with the Hendrix estate, it became clear that it would simplify matters greatly if we were to drop the "Jimi Hendrix Museum" name. Though this decision was made with some sense of regret—I think it's safe to say that everyone involved had *truly* wanted to one day see "Jimi Hendrix Museum" emblazoned across the front of whatever building we ended up in—it wasn't long before the upsides of making this change were being gingerly articulated.

One obvious plus would be that the community's Hendrix haters would lose their target. Another advantage was that with a more generalized name, the institution might be more accurately viewed by the public as the inclusive place we intended it to be. And thus, after additional meetings had been held to review what our real goals were, a new name was chosen, one that reflected the founder's truest vision for the whole project: that of helping visitors *experience music*.

That same year the organization's newsletter, *Feedback*, published my essay, "Hunting & Gathering for EMP: A State of the Collections." In part, this update on our activities said, "While EMP has been actively—if rather quietly—hunting and gathering artifacts for a good three years now, EMP has in recent months begun to capture the community's imagination. Through a combination of general media coverage, postings on the Internet site, this newsletter, and increased staff interactions with members of the community,

EMP's goal of achieving a high level of public support is becoming a reality. While our curatorial efforts have largely focused on acquiring artifacts the old-fashioned way—by attending public auctions, haunting flea markets and estate sales, and working the collectors 'underground'—by far the most satisfying method of adding to EMP's collections is when members of the community step forward and offer up their treasured items."

Our sales pitch worked. Over the following years EMP did in fact receive many, many donations from supportive people, both common citizens and famous musicians. Another reason to take delight in the direction we were heading was that the day finally arrived when the team decided on galleries in addition to the central Hendrix exhibit. The formal designation that one be dedicated to Pacific Northwest music history set the corks a-poppin' at a serious champagne festival at Kate's and my house that night.

CAPTURING AURAL HISTORY

In the summer of 1995, it was decided that the EMP team would pay a let's-get-acquainted visit to the staff at the newly opened Rock and Roll Hall of Fame and Museum in Cleveland, Ohio. Over the last couple years members of their staff and ours had made friendly gestures of outreach to each other, so when this trip was proposed, their director, Dennis Barrie, kindly welcomed the idea and off we went. It was early September, and upon our arrival Barrie greeted us, introduced us to the senior staff, and proceeded to guide us through a very informative back-of-the-house tour. We shared a nice lunch and exchanged information about our respective projects.

As with our earlier reconnaissance patrols of peer institutions, we took copious notes on the facility and its functionality. As Neil Strauss would later write of our activity in a *New York Times* essay,

"Two weeks after the Rock and Roll Hall of Fame and Museum opened . . . Paul Allen . . . sent a small contingent there from Seattle to look around. The group spent two days examining the museum top to bottom. 'Then,' recalled Peter Blecha, a member of that expeditionary force, 'we went back to the hotel room and critiqued it.'"

By analyzing both the positive and negative attributes of the Hall of Fame—things like signage, lighting, artifact selection, audio quality, exhibit techniques, multimedia displays, text-label quality, elevator location, traffic flow issues, and visitor services amenities—our team continued to refine a vision for EMP and simultaneously honed our own analytical skills.

After that trip, smaller subsets of our team, including me, repeated the same exercise at other sites, such as the Smithsonian Institution, the Holocaust Museum, and others in Washington, D.C. Then there were trips to New York City's Metropolitan Museum of Art, the Museum of Modern Art, and the Guggenheim Museum. Some of us visited the Lollapalooza Festival in Canada, various Hard Rock Cafes in Vancouver, British Columbia, Nashville, and London, the Sixth Floor Museum at Dallas's Dealey Plaza, the House of Blues club in Cambridge and the new one in West Hollywood, and Bill Graham's corporate offices in San Francisco. In addition, and on an individual basis, I made trips to famous archaeological sites in rural France, and to music shrines like Nashville's Grand Ol' Opry and the Country Music Hall of Fame and Museum. Add to that individual trips to the Museum of Fine Arts, Boston, various historical sites and museums in Philadelphia, the new Guggenheim Museum in Bilbao, Spain, the British Museum in London, and the Louvre and the Musée d'Orsay in Paris. It was a whirlwind education, but hey, anything for the cause, right?

Once the planning team had completed a few rounds of touring such institutions, I'd gained a far more exacting sense of what types of exhibits were being mounted elsewhere. That awareness reassured me and the EMP team that there was still room for our enterprise to successfully carve out a unique niche.

Soon EMP's little team had grown to nine—bolstered by five part-timers and as many as thirty consultants—and the *P-I* wasn't too far off the mark when they noted that "for creative types, the EMP workplace is a dream: Rock rules, the boss has deep pockets, and no idea's too wild." And too, "Like the collection, everything about this museum-in-the-making is massing and morphing on a grand scale . . . Once-modest collections at EMP have snowballed along with the project's scope. Curators working long hours at computers in Bellevue headquarters have 10,000 artifacts catalogued, with a backlog of 5,000 to 6,000, and more on the way."

With exhibit planning due to begin sometime soon, I and others on the team began agitating for the establishment of, as we termed it, an "Oral History Video Documentary project." We felt that the exhibits, whatever they might end up being about, needed to have a media component that included musicians talking on-screen about their art. When finally prompted, Paul and Jody understood and authorized us to begin by seeking advice from some recognized experts. And so we had consultations with Seattle's reigning oral historian, MOHAI's Dr. Lorraine McConaghy, and then with Joan Ringleheim, the director of oral history at the Holocaust Museum.

With a clearer idea of how formal oral histories are produced and organized, we proceeded to book a session with a very high-priority interview subject, Al Hendrix. The camera operator was Joe Vinikow, an award-winning filmmaker who'd been serving as the project team's media consultant, and I was charged with conducting the interview. Al welcomed us into his home and we set up the camera and audio gear in his basement music room—a charming family shrine to Jimi that was heavily postered and even had a few of the late guitarist's guitars and amps lying around. Al pointed to an old couch in the corner and said that it had been around since the 1950s and his son Jimi had taken many a youthful catnap on it. He also pointed out an old record player and stack of discs, noting that they too dated to Jimi's boyhood. Al told us to make ourselves at home and while Vinikow continued adjusting his gear, I yielded to the irresistible temptation to take a few minutes to flip through those records in the hopes of getting a glimpse into the musical tastes of young Jimi. While most of the songs there were typical radio hits from back in the day, what really grabbed my attention were a couple early 45s on the local Seafair Bolo label. To me, this was a nice little bit of physical proof that Jimi had had an awareness of the local bands of his era.

Then, when we were ready to roll, the interview began. I think Al was generally surprised that we were interested in the deep background of his family's Northwest roots. I think it probable that the majority of interviewers Al had accommodated over the years were obsessed with trying to drain every possible factoid about Jimi from him. So, for our interview, he was more than happy to share stories about his parents and grandparents and details about his own youth. Now, it didn't hurt that having interviewed Al plenty in the past, I already knew what his best stories were—and, conversely, what sorts of inquiries were total dead-enders. But this particular session did produce a few new twists as well: partway through, Al jumped up and retrieved a plastic garbage bag from a nearby closet, and started pulling out jumbles of his son's clothing from it. There before us in wrinkled-up wads was such iconic stage attire as the famous rainbow-striped satiny outfit that Jimi had worn at the filmed Isle of Wight concert festival in 1970. Al also had all sorts of recognizable hippie vests, blouses, scarves, the works. Struggling to hide our keen disappointment at the manner in which these items were being stored, we instead calmly reached out and showed him how they'd be better off hung up or neatly folded—beyond that, we offered to help out anytime he wanted by giving him the appropriate acid-free archival conservation paper commonly used for wrapping such treasures. Al seemed to appreciate the advice, and we left with the museum project's first oral history session a success.

With that one interview completed, the team made a convincing case that in order to acquire the necessary interviews to support the EMP's myriad planned exhibits, we needed a team working much more aggressively. Jody asked for a written plan that included a "hit list" of potential targets. I began loosely categorizing names into four groups that seemed to represent the topical areas the museum would eventually want to cover in various exhibits—Hendrix-related, Northwest hit-makers, guitar masters, and roots-music icons.

Bob Scheu and I developed an operating plan that suggested hiring freelance camera operators, a lighting technician, a photographer, and an audio engineer. The plan was eventually approved and our *Feedback* newsletter was soon quoting me about this new effort: "It is our goal to have the creators of the music—the musicians, recording engineers, and producers—present all this great music history at the museum themselves, where and whenever possible. After all, it's their music and their lives. EMP believes that they should have the chance to tell their own stories in their own words. To this end, we have assembled a fine young crew of experienced video-production artists who have begun interviewing luminaries of the music world so that their knowledge, remembrances, and insights can be shared with museum visitors forever."

Guided by the hit list (while also remaining open to other opportunities that arose), we finally began shooting interviews in earnest. Over the next few years we conducted well over two hundred interview sessions with a vast field of creative musicians, including guitarists such as Les Paul, Chet Atkins, Buck Owens, Buddy Guy, John Mayall, Larry Coryell, Lonnie Mack, Elvin Bishop, Marty Stuart, and Brent Mason. Northwest luminaries included Quincy Jones, Floyd Standifer, Ernestine Anderson, Bonnie Guitar, Bud Tutmarc, and members of local bands like the Ventures, the Wailers, Little Bill and the Bluenotes, the Kingsmen, Merrilee Rush and the Turnabouts, Heart, Pearl Jam, Mudhoney, Tad, Mad Season, and Nirvana.

Other notable stars were Lionel Hampton, Lowell Fulson, Big Jay McNeely, Henry Rollins, and Ice-T.

I took much personal pleasure in arranging for professionally videotaped interviews with all of the local musicians—after all, I'd already interviewed most of them a time or two in past years, but never before on camera or with a skilled audio engineer helping capture their memories. With these new sessions it really seemed like we were finally doing definitive interviews for posterity.

A lot of these sessions remain indelible memories, both for the spirited conversations that ensued and for the interesting settings where they occurred. There was my interview with the West Coast's 1940s and 1950s "Deacon of the Blues," that trailblazing tenor sax honker Big Jay McNeely, which we held in one of central LA's last genuine old-time R&B joints, Babe's and Ricky's Inn out on Leimert Boulevard. Another was the wonderful session with my all-time favorite local singer/guitarist, Bonnie Guitar, that was set in a log-cabin lodge at Soap Lake, Washington. That same night she put our crew on her guest list at a basement-level nightclub and, as such a fine hostess, proceeded to take sixteen of my favorite country-western song requests in a row, playing each and every one with perfect grace. I'll also never forget the session with rapper Ice-T that was held in an empty warehouse on some Hollywood backlot, and was squeezed in between takes he was filming for the *Law and Order: SVU* TV show.

But if one single interview encounter stands out as the most memorable, I think it would have to be the one with a famous 1950s rock 'n' roller whose name—for reasons I trust y'all will understand—probably shouldn't even be mentioned here. Did I say memorable? *Oh yeah!* After a fine interview—in which he plugged in his original guitar and showed off his still amazingly dexterous skills—this guy then allowed me and other crew members to each have a thrilling shot at playing the historic instrument. Loud! But that was only the beginning of the fun. After he pressured us into staying over for dinner at his Deep South backwoods cabin, he further proved to be the model host by jumping in his ol' pickup, racing off down the gravel road, and returning fifteen minutes later with a mason jar plumb full of something I'd sure never seen, or tasted, before: 100 percent pure Tennessee moonshine. Needless to say, even we Seattle city slickers let out a rebel yell or two *that* night!

Plenty of fun was certainly had by many of the EMP staffers besides me who got involved in these oral history shoots, but on a more serious note, I think we all shared a sober sense that in the very collecting of them we were helping produce a unique archive of captured memories—memories that would richly augment the museum's eventual exhibits and permanent research archives.

▶ A 1934 example of the first electric guitar to hit the marketplace: a "Rickenbacher" Electro Hawaiian A-25 "Frying Pan" lap steel.

GALLERIES, GUITARS & GOODIES

TESTING THE TEAM

Although it was perhaps obvious only to people paying close attention to such things, the Hard Rock Cafes and Cleveland's Rock and Roll Hall of Fame were worlds apart in their presentation styles. But their exhibits *did* share a focus on the "superstars" of rock history. And while that formula was a proven winner, our planning for EMP began to lead in significantly different directions (though let's face it, that EMP would have a core Hendrix exhibit was a major comforting ace up our sleeve).

Rather than just celebrate the overachievers of the music biz, EMP saw value in trying to help demystify the workings of the music industry. The guiding principle of the museum would be to create exhibits that shone a spotlight on the admittedly abstract concepts of "creativity" and "innovation" in music. EMP hoped to engage future visitors with exhibits that might, for example, illuminate how an entire music scene develops; how musicians use various tools to invent innovative sounds; how artists find and channel creative inspiration; how songs are created; and how some songs are turned into hits. Ambitious and complex goals, no doubt, but we thought them more rewarding than simply mounting cool artifacts in exhibits, à la the Hard Rock Cafes—whose message seemed to be "Here's the cool rock 'n' roll stuff you paid to see. Now buy a burger, sucker."

As we churned through ideas, we developed a prioritized exhibit list, deciding on at least six distinct and discrete gallery spaces for the eventual new building: (1) the Jimi Hendrix Gallery; (2) a gallery for the Northwest's regional music history; (3) a gallery that focused on the tools musicians use to make their art (or, as it finally took form, a display of electric-guitar history); (4) a gallery called Crossroads, featuring rotating exhibits about various aspects of music culture; (5) a space called the Soundlab, in which visitors could interact with instruments and other music-making devices; and (6) a temporary gallery for mounting loaned materials or traveling shows on a short-term basis.

These decisions had an immediate impact on every member of the team, especially the collections and curatorial staff. In order to mount such a range of displays, we curators needed to broaden and accelerate the acquisition of artifacts. By March 1996, EMP had informed the media that the museum had seventeen thousand items logged into its database—but much of that was archival materials relating to Hendrix and the Northwest. Artifacts intended to support any other exhibits would still need to be collected.

As the assigning of tasks commenced, my responsibilities for building the Hendrix and Northwest collections were augmented by those of building an instrument collection to support the guitar-history gallery. Truth be told, I volunteered for this last task and actually had the most fun with it. That's partially because I'd been involved in collecting both Hendrix and Northwest materials for such a long time that taking on a new area was refreshing. Not that I was a total neophyte: as far back as my high school years—when I'd been learning guitar in addition to drumming—I'd had an eye for interesting vintage string instruments. My own collection included an 1890s folk-art mandolin, a few turn-of-the-nineteenth-century harps, a circa 1912 banjo, a 1941 Epiphone electric tenor guitar, my trusty old 1964 Gibson LG-1, and a number of 1930s electric lap steels.

Still, even though I'd collected these gems and I'd been attending Seattle's Guitar Show for a number of years, I was most certainly no expert. But I was willing to immerse myself and learn everything I could about guitar history. So the intensive research began. I read every book I could lay my hands on. I picked the brains of knowledgeable local musicians and guitar collector friends. I spent a lot of time hanging out in area guitar shops, jabbering with the proprietors and their fix-it men and sales staff. I started attending some of the country's really great guitar shows in places like Dallas, St. Louis, Nashville, Los Angeles, and Portland. I met many of the top dealers, as well as lots of manufacturer reps, and I befriended a good number of subject specialists. And along the way, I steadily built up an informational archive of clippings about the earliest history of guitars and amplifiers, and their makers.

I realized fairly early on that the museum's guitar collection wouldn't be just any random assortment of guitars. It couldn't just be old guitars, or pretty guitars, or big guitars, or some such. In order to fulfill the museum's mandate of tracking creativity and innovation, the collection had to represent the most *significant* milestones in the entire design history of the instrument. The eventual exhibit would have to be capable of conveying, particularly to an uninitiated visitor, the long chain of accumulated innovations in guitar design that had led, over at least 250 years, to that perfect rock 'n' roll tool: the electric guitar.

I felt compelled to learn exactly who (or which guitar companies) had actually contributed what to the evolutionary advancement of this instrument, and so I studied and charted the achievements of every notable luthier (guitar maker) or designer from the 1700s on. It became apparent that in order to introduce this subject in display form to the general public, an exhibit would need to accomplish several things. Ideally, it would establish the origins of the guitar as an ancient string instrument, probably hailing from Spain's Iberian Peninsula. The exhibit would show how the instrument was further developed and refined in France and Italy. We'd show how luthiers came up with varying innovative guitar designs in order to, among other things, make the instruments louder. Then we'd represent the late 1920s and early 1930s, when a few visionary inventors began tinkering with electricity and guitars. In a process known to academics as "independent co-generation," these makers came up with differing ways of electrifying formerly acoustic instruments, thus launching the sonic revolution spearheaded by what we all now know as electric guitars.

As this basic storyline came into focus, so too did the monumental challenge I faced in actualizing an exhibit that would adequately represent what was an incredibly tangled history. It seemed that in order to convey guitar history fairly, we would require at minimum a few very early pre-electric acoustic guitars—perhaps an ancient European specimen—and then an American-made Gibson and Martin from the 1800s. In addition, my wish list included an array of the earliest electrics made by the pioneering firms of Rickenbacker, Dobro, Audiovox, Vivi-Tone, National, Slingerland, and Gibson. And beyond needing prime examples of the triumvirate of perfected electrics—the Fender Telecaster, the Gibson Les Paul, and Fender Stratocaster—I also hoped to nail down museum-quality examples of a 1940s Bigsby, a Gibson Flying V, a Rickenbacker electric twelve-string, a Fender Jazzmaster, a Gretsch Country Gentleman, an Ovation, and a few dramatically ultramodern, "cutting-edge" guitars (exact makes and models to be determined). Within two years I had reeled in a remarkable, if still small, collection of prime specimens of some of the earliest (and most significant) electric guitars ever designed and built. If my gig at EMP had seemed like a dream job before, well, this new guitar gallery "chore" greatly enhanced that perception.

During 1996 further changes were occurring with the museum's structure, as the vision for it continued to expand. It was in this year that EMP announced the hiring of renowned architect Frank Gehry to design a museum building. With this hiring, the grand opening was pushed back to 1999. In 1996 the museum team was also challenged with a major test: to develop a temporary exhibit to be mounted thirty miles south of Seattle at the old Tacoma Art Museum (TAM). Our years of collecting artifacts would finally see fruition in an array of historically oriented displays that would be mini versions of what EMP might become. The team brainstormed ideas for the specific exhibit components and my fellow curator, Jim Fricke, and I immediately collaborated on selecting Hendrix-related artifacts. Our goal for this part of the show was to tell of Jimi's early local roots, his climb to fame, and his eventual conquering of the rock 'n' roll world between 1967 and 1970.

The team also had to figure out a way to tie all this together in a coherent, meaningful presentation—along with additional non-Hendrix exhibits. I had already begun developing the guitar-history exhibit. I had also been working on two other exhibits: one that represented the pioneering days of Northwest rock 'n' roll and another that celebrated the accomplishments of the grunge generation.

A guitar-history portion seemed a natural tangent for the Hendrix exhibit: anyone who liked Hendrix, the Kingsmen, the Sonics, and the other 1960s rockers or grunge music probably would have at least some interest in the origin of the electric guitar. As for the bookend stories of local rock history, it seemed that we could easily draw some interesting connections between the seminal sounds of the early 1960s and the more-famous "Seattle Sound" of recent years. Taking it one step further, I figured we could make a link between Hendrix growing up listening to Northwest music of the "Louie Louie" era, and then moving on to influence his own generation through his music, which in turn filtered down to the musicians of today.

I was convinced that the intellectual underpinnings of this little "test" exhibit were probably valid, but I also knew that it was the *quality* of our artifacts that would blow people away. The wow factor of the Hendrix materials was, of course, a given. But another secret weapon would be the grunge goods I'd hauled in. Sure, there would be all sorts of early posters, records, and photographs of Pearl Jam, Soundgarden, and other well-known grunge bands, but the real icing on the cake would be the sunburst Fender Stratocaster formerly owned and played by the late Kurt Cobain of Nirvana.

This was a fascinating-looking instrument with an even more interesting backstory. I'd acquired it through the New York–based Guernsey's auction house. The lot I bid on also included some Florida newspaper clippings that documented how some lucky local kid had acquired the guitar after Cobain pulled him up on stage out of the mosh pit and let this guy help him bash the thing around. Then, when Nirvana finished that song, they invited this kid backstage, where all three band members autographed the instrument—an instrument that, lucky for us, he soon decided to sell through Guernsey's.

Strange as it may sound, I was now developing a curatorial fondness for *ruined* guitars. Guitars that had been destroyed in concert by some rock star—and goodness knows, everyone from Hendrix to the Who to the Clash to Nirvana had wrecked a bunch of them—actually had some visual attraction that pristine instruments lacked. A destructive incident that resulted in a battered or broken instrument offered a tie to the historical place and time of a particular concert. And this Cobain Strat provided a wealth of interesting features. It was beaten and bruised from a violent assault. Cracked down the middle, the guitar also had broken strings dangling from it. It was, as mentioned, inscribed by the band. And one more thing: it also had a few small speckles of Cobain's blood on it. This is nothing unusual for a guitar played by an aggressive rock 'n' roller: plenty of players nick their hands in performance and shed traces on their strings or pickguards. Still, given Cobain's passing less than a year prior, this minor detail caught the imagination of the media vultures, who publicized the guitar with unrestrained and incredibly tasteless descriptions such as "blood soaked" and "blood drenched."

After much preparation, Strats, Studios, and the Seattle Sound opened at TAM on July 13, 1996, and between then and September 8, around eighty thousand visitors came—a figure that reportedly far outstripped earlier attendance records at that museum. Rock fans flocked to see Hendrix's white Woodstock Strat and Kurt Cobain's "blood-soaked" guitar, along with everything else we presented, and media coverage was glowing. EMP's leadership seemed very pleased with all the work the team had done, and I think the entire museum staff felt major relief at seeing that our exhibit concepts were accepted and enjoyed by the public—that all the ideas we'd been jawboning about for so long were becoming *achievable*.

Indeed, Strats, Studios, and the Seattle Sound proved to be such a hit that we were soon invited to mount a reprise in Seattle at the Pacific Science Center. Running from December 13, 1996, through January 20, 1997, the show once again caught the public's attention. After this trial run the team turned to the far greater task at hand: developing the much bigger and more complex exhibits that would comprise the actual inaugural displays for EMP.

WIRED WOOD

In late 1996, with general museum planning roaring full steam ahead, esteemed musicologist, longtime *New York Times* critic, and contributing editor at *Rolling Stone* Robert Palmer was brought onboard the EMP team. Palmer and I hit it off immediately, enjoying deep discussions about the African roots of the rock 'n' roll impulse, the importance of Hendrix, and other topics. In particular, Palmer showed an interest in my off-hours research on the global history of music censorship (a topic I would—much later—write a book about). It wasn't too long before he fell into his stride at the project and proposed that, in order to establish the scholarly credentials of EMP, we launch a publication program. In particular, Palmer felt we should begin with a formal monograph series that he would guide and edit.

As it happened, an essay—*Wired Wood: The Origins of the Electric Guitar*—that I'd been shaping while organizing the guitar exhibit was chosen to be the monograph series' first imprint. As I'd peeled back the saga behind these instruments while developing the guitar exhibit, their story had coalesced in my mind as a fairly streamlined path. *Wired Wood* represented my attempts to articulate this arc of innovation on paper. Though my writings on various other topics had been published in a number of different magazines, this would be the closest that I'd yet come to publishing something like a book— or, really, a booklet. I was thrilled.

The moment I received the first copies of *Wired Wood*, I shipped some as gifts to a number of the top guitar historians in the country, as a gesture of gratitude for their help during my research. I was pleased when several of these acquaintances responded with enthusiasm to my apparently different approach to electric-guitar history. Typically, other authors had written about long-standing interests in some particular brand of guitar, be it Gibson, Rickenbacker, Fender, or whatever. The common result was a tale that tilted toward favoring one of these pioneering firms over all the others.

My angle—really that of a drummer who happened to be fascinated with guitars as objects of physical beauty and milestones of technological design history—had been a bit purer. Without a dog in the fight, I could be more objective. Bringing fresh eyes to the matter, my only goal was to try and untangle all the conflicting legends and claims behind just exactly *who* invented *what*. I confess that after getting the seal of approval from experts such as George Gruhn, I felt relieved.

In fact, Gruhn was impressed enough with my examination of the technological issues associated with the development of the electric guitar that he passed along a copy of *Wired Wood* to a friend. Gruhn's friend, it turned out, was Professor Nicholas Toth, a co-director of the Indiana University–based Center for Research into the Anthropological Foundations of Technology (CRAFT).

Toth—also a musician, vintage-guitar enthusiast, and one of the world's premier flintknappers (modern makers of prehistoric-style stone tools)—read the monograph and, after we engaged in a number of rollicking and wide-ranging conversations about everything from rocks to rock 'n' roll, he invited me to join the CRAFT Advisory Board. CRAFT already included some renowned and respected scientists (along with an extremely eclectic array of other folks, including Gruhn, environmental artist Henry Corning, newsman Walter Cronkite, and *Clan of the Cave Bear* author Jean Auel). I must admit, at first I felt a bit out of my league—but, handed this opportunity, I could hardly decline. I figured, when else in life would I—the serial college dropout and un-degreed amateur cultural anthropologist—*ever* have the chance to associate with such learned people?

Perhaps Toth viewed my long dedication to researching Northwest regional music history (at a time when almost *nothing* had been published on the topic) as a sort of anthropological quest, not unlike how other scientists have uncovered and documented forgotten or lost societies in strange corners of the world. I don't really know. What seemed certain was that this was my chance to dive into the deep end of the pool and probably learn plenty about the state-of-the-art anthropological and archaeological work being conducted at various CRAFT sites around the world. If any of these people figured that I had anything to contribute to their discussions, well, *cool*—just add this new thrill to my life's tally of unexpected though perfectly welcomed plot twists.

Since I joined up I've enjoyed being briefed about various important field projects CRAFT has under way, guest-lecturing in one of Toth's classes at Indiana University, and attending, whenever possible, annual board meetings. There have also been fascinating gatherings where the assembled can review CRAFT's ongoing fieldwork and discuss future goals for the organization and funding strategies. Such sessions have taken me to places like Paris and the Bordeaux region of France, San Sebastian, Spain, and a sunny beachside villa at a private bay on Saint Thomas in the Caribbean.

It's a credit to CRAFT—recently renamed the Stone Age Institute—that the organization has drawn such a diverse array of people to its board. While some members participate because they bring direct experience as premier scientists in their fields, others of us contribute in less obvious ways. I'd guess that I've been welcomed because

I know just enough about anthropology and archaeology to not drag down discussions, but also bring to the table a keen awareness about both pop culture and the nature of invention and innovation—this along with the ability to, on occasion, tie observations about these disparate realms together in some meaningful way.

GROUNDBREAKING DEVELOPMENTS

On the sunny afternoon of June 13, 1997, a fun public ground breaking was held at EMP's Seattle Center construction site. Beyond all the usual pomp and circumstance of speeches and ceremonial dirt shoveling, the real joy was watching Seattle's legendary radio DJ Pat O'Day introduce spirited performances by Northwest bands, including the Kingsmen, Mudhoney, and the hottest new rockers in the city at that time, the Presidents of the United States of America.

Even at that momentous day's end, the excitement didn't subside one bit. Just as legions of workers began their massive three-year construction process the next day, so did the curatorial team begin laying the foundations for the final forms of our planned exhibits.

The Hendrix exhibit had made steady progress and was shaping up nicely, and the guitar exhibit, too, looked to be on track—although the search for guitars wasn't nearly over yet. But it was the Northwest exhibit that had me worried. You see, by this time—perhaps two full years into hunting down and gathering Northwest-related music artifacts—I had brought several thousand records, posters, magazines, and other materials into EMP's collections. But even with those materials flowing in, it was becoming ever more apparent that the glory days of digging up local memorabilia had probably passed. Unlike earlier times, by the mid-1990s there were hordes of other collectors actively scouring for the same stuff, and day by day it was getting harder to locate museum-quality rarities.

While EMP was assembling an unrivaled archive of recent, grunge/post-grunge-era artifacts, it was proving difficult to find worthy examples of basic Northwest classics like, say, Kingsmen or Sonics albums. The former—probably because they'd all been played to death at fraternity parties—were turning up only in ratty and unexhibitable condition; and the latter, if they turned up at all, were commanding prices up to $300—plus they were not necessarily in exhibitable shape. Finding anything rarer than these was largely a hit-or-miss proposition. And the clock was ticking.

Faced with these obstacles, I realized that the success of EMP's collection-development efforts was actually beyond our own control. I could not, in truth, ensure the team that our Northwest collection would have a suitably large selection of artifacts before the deadline.

In order to create the high-quality displays required, I expressed a willingness, should it prove necessary, to loan *some* items from my own collection to the museum. But, while we wanted EMP's Northwest history exhibit to be the finest possible, I wasn't too comfortable with the idea of loaning large quantities of my best material to a display that might very well stay up for years on end. I mentioned to Jody that if EMP leadership ever thought they might want to consider the option, I would be willing to sell my beloved collection to the museum.

Given the size and quality of my own personal collection, their interest was piqued. Eventually I was asked to prepare a specific proposal. While that was to be no easy task, at least I had a head start from the inventory Kate and I had done. We knew that the nearly twenty thousand artifacts held a current market value of X dollars. And because I'd so truly wanted to see the whole thing go to a good home one day, I played no games in preparing the proposal document. I didn't round up my estimated evaluation total. I didn't bluff or exaggerate. I just reported what I had, and what its street value was out in the collectors' world.

After presenting the proposal, some time went by, and all the while I just kept at the job of mining my sources and pulling in more Northwest items—even if they duplicated what was already in my collection. Then, one glorious day in July 1997, I was informed that the sale was approved. This was a huge deal in my life. I would soon be biting the bullet and handing off a collection I'd worked to build for more than two decades. My long-standing dreams for the collection were actually coming true. I'd successfully developed a museum-quality collection; I felt strongly that I'd helped raise my community's awareness about the real value of our often-overlooked collective music history; and I'd reached the final goal of seeing that collection enter an institutional repository where it would be safe, attended to by professional conservationists, logged into a database by professional information specialists, and housed where it would benefit future researchers and the general public.

Perhaps the most significant contribution that any collector can make to the greater good is that of providing the public service of historical preservation. This accomplishment can occur only if the collection stays intact and ultimately finds a public role. With this sale, I believed deeply that this criterion was met, and I will forever feel some pride whenever I see items from my old collection integrated into various displays at EMP. I hope that my former collection will long serve as an important cornerstone of the museum's archives.

Now, while I can't say there weren't plenty of second thoughts and nervous misgivings about concluding the transaction, the truth is that letting it all go was a bit therapeutic. Actually owning my collection had come to be overwhelming. Like plenty of collectors before me, I had over time begun to feel an aching responsibility for the physical *safety* of all this stuff. That I had a small fortune invested in the collection was barely a factor in this unease. Because the collection comprised such a unique assemblage of historical materials, I was beginning to feel the "weight of the community" on my shoulders.

Although most of the town had no idea that I was husbanding "our" history, I was starting to get, well, a bit wiggy about having it all stowed unprotected down in the basement. When Kate and I would leave even for a weekend getaway, I'd worry about it. I'd become so compulsive that as I left the house for work each day, I'd typically find myself triple-checking that the doorknobs were locked, eyeballing various window latches to verify that they were all set, and glancing around to see if any mysterious vehicles were parked nearby—and this was in addition to the professional home burglar alarm system we'd had installed! That it was somewhat inconceivable that anyone could have stolen—or even would have *wanted* to steal—twenty thousand Northwest relics didn't matter to me.

The day soon came when several fellow members of EMP's collections staff arrived at our house with a big truck. We packed everything into shipping crates, I said my farewells, and like a parent whose kid just moved out, I felt a keen emptiness.

But from my viewpoint as EMP's senior curator, I was elated. With my former collection added to the thousands of Northwest items I'd already brought into EMP's vault, the combination instantly amounted to the finest archive of its type imaginable. While EMP's collection had been heavy on recent grunge-era artifacts, my collection balanced things out by adding items that represented the deeper history of our region. And EMP was happy to send me out to talk up the new and improved Northwest collection with any reporter who took an interest in our progress. As *The Rocket* later reported, "Pete Blecha estimates that half the artifacts owned by EMP are Northwest related—an accomplishment he is very proud of. 'It's a tremendous, unparalleled regional archive. Our goal is to show locals and tourists that while we're known for grunge and "Louie Louie" there's a great range and depth of music that has come out of the Northwest over the years.'"

JIMI HENDRIX: THE COLLECTOR

The ongoing effort to build EMP's Hendrix collection was an exhilarating campaign, though we encountered the occasional hitch. In the early days—before I had been formally authorized to lead the quest for acquisitions—the few of us involved in curatorial matters were invited to submit an opinion about whether or not (and why) some Hendrix artifact listed in an auction catalog would be desirable. When the general consensus was that we wanted the item, we'd hash out a maximum bidding cap—one that had a decent chance of success, but that was within reasonable limits of the known marketplace value range.

This is how, at the very beginning, I acquired a few *very* significant Hendrix-related collectibles. One notable lot was a remarkable group of 128 records from Jimi's very own LP collection that was sold through Sotheby's by his British girlfriend, Kathy Etchingham. For some reason, she had divided Jimi's records into a couple lots. Many observers had been surprised when the first batch of 26 had sold at Bonham's for $1,800. *That*, people in the record-collecting world hissed, was nearly $70 apiece—and for records that were in very poor condition. Hendrix collectors far and wide gossiped about what a sucker the anonymous buyer had been. I disagreed and regretted that the museum project hadn't been fully on top of the situation in time to grab them ourselves.

Thankfully, the batch of 128 popped up later at Sotheby's. This time we were better prepared, and that much larger lot went to us for just over $3,000—only to spark complaints that this was an undervalued figure, with one London publication bemoaning that EMP had paid a "paltry" sum for them. I had to agree: at something around $25 per disc, it had been a total bargain. London's *Mojo* magazine quoted me on the discs' intrinsic value to EMP: they were "a genuine treasure trove that offers a priceless lens with which we can gain a bit more insight into the musical mind of one of the 20th century's most profound musicians."

When the lot was shipped to us and I was able to examine it, one fact became clear: this was a great opportunity to study exactly what recorded music Jimi chose to surround himself with during his London days. As I stated in *Mojo*, "Jimi had a tremendous interest in other musicians' explorations. Among these records are seminal blues recordings that helped form the roots of Jimi's own sound. There's essential R&B stuff like James Brown that one would hope to find, as well as the jazz that Jimi was supposedly developing a deeper interest in. Also represented are some of his heroes and friends like Bob Dylan, Santana, and Albert King. There's also British music, like the Beatles and Cream, that helped draw Hendrix to London in the first place, a couple nods to his hometown heavies, Ray Charles and Larry Coryell (Free Spirits). And there's radio pop, like the Bee Gees, Motown, and Simon & Garfunkel."

Though I'd seen and handled other copies of all these records before, there was something very cool—almost spiritual—about knowing that Jimi Hendrix himself had collected, owned, played, and *loved* this music. And although in my earlier retail career I'd handled records weeded out of other Northwest rock stars' collections, this case was a truly unique and educational opportunity to study a batch of them—still almost undisturbed—as a *collection*.

STONE FREE

Try as I might to spread the word that the museum wasn't in the business of wildly throwing money around, some people just didn't get it. Without a doubt the creepiest offer came when I found myself engaged in a phone conversation with a very nervous-sounding fellow who started out by tentatively saying something like, "I have this thing and I can't really tell you what it is. But: it's something that Paul Allen will want for his Hendrix museum."

After a bit of reassurance that our conversation would be handled in the utmost confidence, the caller loosened up enough to tell his story. "Well, OK: I'm not proud of this, but many years ago, I did a bad thing. Remember when Jimi Hendrix's headstone went missing from his gravesite?" I was stunned. I remembered that a few years after Jimi's 1970 burial at Greenwood Memorial Park in Renton, Washington, his headstone had been pried up, stolen, and soon thereafter replaced.

"Well, I was a young man then, and I'm the one who . . . took it. Now I'm older, a family man, and seriously ill. I'm dying. And I have two young daughters whose future I'm worried about—and so I need to sell it to you."

This was certainly one for the books—at least *this* book. Normally fairly fast on the draw, this particular time I paused to take a deep breath before responding. Not because I was thinking of how to pull this deal off—it was entirely outside the realm of possibility, not to mention professional and legal ethics, for the museum to acquire a stolen object. Besides, our planned exhibit for Jimi was intended to be a celebration of his creativity and his musical *life*—we had no possible context in which to exhibit a headstone.

No, what I had to quickly come up with was a response to a fellow human being who faced serious problems: health problems, family problems, but most of all, moral problems. So I told him, "Sir, first of all this museum will not be buying that headstone from you. I understand that given your health concerns you have a real need to try and establish some means of providing ongoing financial support for your daughters. But the headstone is technically stolen property. I feel that I can only advise you as to what I think is the proper action for you to take—and that would be to make contact with the Hendrix estate and offer to find a way to return it to them, perhaps in an anonymous fashion. I'm sure that they would work with you to see that occur in a way that settles the matter in an honorable way for everybody."

He definitely didn't agree and gave no indication that he would follow through with the suggestion, but at least I'd tried. And, truth be told, I'd felt a little like Ward Cleaver having to mildly chastise the Beav, but that was that and I never heard from him again. I shared that story with workmates as well as friends, and everyone seemed to gain a new appreciation for the types of challenges that came along as part of my job.

THE JIMI HENDRIX TREE

Even so, no encounters could ever compete with the total weirdness of another phoned-in solicitation. This incident, I must confess, is shared mainly at my own expense; it's a telling of what was probably the most prominent (and embarrassing) faux pas I ever committed in my years at EMP.

The incident occurred in the mid-1990s, early enough into my association with the relatively new e-mail technology that allowed forwarding of messages to other employees' *voice mail*. Although I usually avoided bothering other people around the office by sharing my business, in this one case I made the fateful error of being far too generous with a hilarious message I'd received—and that act became a legendary in-house blunder.

One day a caller left me a voice mail unlike any I've heard before or since: "Hello? Uh, Mr. Bellka? Hey, this is Billy Crawford calling, and I gotta tell you, I've got something down here that Mr. Allen is going to want for his Jimi Hendrix museum—*for sure*—and I'm just wonderin' if you could call me about it? You know, I'm certain that if Mr. Allen could just come down to my house down here in Renton he'd take one look and just know he *had* to get this thing into his museum. See, I'm sitting out here in my backyard and I just happened to notice that when the sun shines through my tree it casts a shadow on the garage wall—and it looks just like Jimi Hendrix. Only, it's not just a shadow . . . it's the *spirit* of Jimi Hendrix. *I'm not kidding you*. It *is* Jimi Hendrix. And so, I know that if you and Mr. Allen'd come over and take a look, I *guarantee* he'd want to buy the tree. So hurry and call me back at 555-1234 . . . OK?"

Now that was certainly worth a few laughs. After a few more playbacks and dumbfounded guffaws, I decided to share this with my co-workers, figuring they might enjoy hearing from just *one* of the weirdoes that I had to deal with *every* day. For the first time ever, I clicked the "Forward All" button on my e-mail program—effectively sharing this voice message with every single employee at EMP. Then for good measure I clicked "Vulcan All," adding every single employee of the entire business management group. Instantly hundreds of people had been brought into the loop, from Paul and Jody on down to the receptionists.

Within minutes, a good number of people—those I already knew, and some I didn't—responded favorably, e-mailing back what a total hoot they thought this hillbilly dude was. I figured the little outreach gesture had been a success. But what I hadn't factored in was the possible response of our brand-new multimedia team, who were just dying to take our oral-history program's video gear into the field. And boy did they get keyed up. Who could blame them: this Billy Crawford sounded like a genuine, classic, acid-damaged Hendrix nut. I'd seen and met plenty, and he seemed to fit the profile to a T. Curious about seeing this tree thing myself, even I joined in, agreeing that, yes, a video shoot of this guy—though it's not clear how we'd *ever* actually use it in the Hendrix Gallery—might be a good idea.

That evening when I returned home, I told Kate all about it and we had a good chuckle—hey, just another day in Jimi World. The next day this video shoot idea began picking up momentum and turned into an actual plan. But that night, Kate's mood was a little subdued. She soon informed me that our longtime friend, Ken (an IBM exec), had called up earlier just to check in and see what was new. After they chatted briefly, Ken dropped his bombshell: "Oh, Kate, did Pete tell you about the voice mail message I left him yesterday? I know Pete is always getting ludicrous calls from freaks trying to sell crap to the museum, so I just improvised some bit about a Hendrix Tree." Silence. Kate's pretty swift on the uptake, but it still took her a moment or two to add things up. Then she said, "Ken, you need to talk to Pete when he gets in a little later."

A couple hours later I arrived home and, sure enough, the phone rang. It was Ken: "Hey, Pete. So, how'd you like that message I left you about the Hendrix Tree?" Silence again as my brain struggled to connect the dots. Finally I said, "Ken . . . please tell me that's not true. Oh *shit!*" I was stunned by the realization that I'd been totally taken in by this friend's prank—and by the fact, which I promptly shared with him, that I'd reacted by disseminating that wacky message throughout the whole company. Furthermore, the entire EMP video team was currently gearing up to go shoot an interview with that geek, er, him.

That's when Ken's end of the phone went silent before he said, "No . . . Pete, you didn't do *that*, did you? Oh, no! I think I left my IBM office number in that message!" "Yes, you did Ken," I replied. "And now EMP's team will probably soon be calling you there to set up your interview." Both of us were perfectly mortified. With Ken muttering something about "plausible deniability," my mind was racing to figure how to put this toothpaste back in the tube.

Not only was the Hendrix Tree Nut the talk of the office all week, but the video team was set to go out and capture this guy's tale. Luck interceded, however, when a series of more crucial interview opportunities suddenly arose, so the team never did follow up with "Mr. Crawford."

OL' PIZZA FACE

Every week, it seemed, some "artist" made contact with an offer to paint, build a stained-glass, or cast a bronze-statue tribute to Hendrix—with the caveat that EMP must commit to displaying it permanently at the museum. Such offers—based on this unacceptable contingency—were regularly declined. I figured that if any artist felt such an overriding need to express his/her admiration for Jimi by producing some piece of artwork, great. On rare occasions, we did actually buy such items. But no credible arts institution can agree to permanently exhibiting *anything*—especially an as-yet-unmade and therefore unseen object. Handling all of these solicitations was yet another fun part of the job.

I once received a call from a couple students, Jon Leahy and Mike Fitzpatrick, from the College of William and Mary in Virginia. They wanted us to be aware of a so-called Hendrix-related item that they had. Always interested, I asked them to tell me more. To quote their campus newspaper, the *College Press Exchange*, they had "drafted a drawing of Hendrix's face with the logo colors from dozens of Chanello's Pizza boxes cluttering their room." Initially my mind reeled at the conjured vision of this piece of "artwork" being made by some dorm rats out of their unrecycled trash. More painful were thoughts of the ridicule I would face from fellow staffers if I dared propose that we accept an "artifact" made out of greasy cheese and pepperoni–encrusted cardboard boxes—and, far worse, thoughts of having it stored in our vault with all the precious items we'd already gathered. Nevertheless, there was something undeniably intriguing about the whole situation, and so I asked that they mail over some more information for further consideration. In fact, my curiosity about it was genuine because I'd long ago learned that you really never know: perhaps the darn thing might actually prove to be visually interesting.

Within days a press release accompanied by some professional-quality photographs of the artwork—named *6X9* after Hendrix's song "If 6 Was 9"—arrived in the mail and I was bowled over. It was, in fact, a wonderful 7-by-7-foot abstract collage of pizza-box parts arranged to look like Jimi Hendrix—perhaps not so closely as the legendary Hendrix Tree purportedly did, but very artfully nevertheless. The piece was thoroughly unique. It was attractive and to me seemed an oddly appropriate work of heartfelt tribute to a long-gone artist by some young fans who hadn't even been born when Hendrix had passed on. As such, I saw it as a visual testament to the guitarist's lasting impact. And my worst-case scenario fears were quite misplaced, as the thing appeared clean and free from rodent-attracting food-product stains.

I walked the photos up and down EMP's halls and sought opinions from my workmates. It managed to charm everyone, and we decided that "old pizza face" was in fact something that could easily find a place in some museum exhibit one day. I called the student-artists back and gave them the verdict: we loved their work and would be honored to accept it as a gift. As I explained to the *College Press Exchange*, the main quality I saw in *6X9* was that of a modern example of folk art—a fine example of something beautiful created by untrained people who had a true passion for the task.

Our donors were thrilled and promptly offered to deliver it in person. Their plan was to grab a couple more school buddies and make a madcap cross-country drive with a truck and U-Haul trailer to Seattle. But first they launched a savvy fund-raising scheme that quickly won support from Chanello's Pizza, earned news coverage on MTV, and garnered articles in *Guitar World* and *Experience Hendrix* magazines. The guys finally arrived at our offices one summer day in 1998. They presented *6X9* to EMP as a gift, we filled out the donation paperwork, and I gratefully took them all out for lunch—to a pizza joint, of course!

THE MASTER'S TAPES

Ohe day I was contacted by a guy in London who presented himself as the agent for a seller who was interested in parting with a "fantastic" lot of Hendrix-related materials. Specifically, they had a cache of the nineteen original reel-to-reel master tapes for Hendrix's famous Band of Gypsys concerts from 1969's New Year's Eve weekend at Fillmore East in New York City. Though a killer record from that show had been issued back in 1970, being a single disc, it didn't contain even a fraction of the songs performed at the four different concerts on those dates. I was assured the unreleased material was equally outstanding.

As a fan this was all terribly fascinating, but as a museum agent the first matter of concern was a very basic one: it was the Hendrix estate that held all legal rights to the deceased musician's "name, likeness, and image." It was they, *not* EMP, who had the ability to market and profit from any potential future release of any such recordings. But over weeks of continuing discussions, this fellow offered up the intriguing tidbit that he had previously entered into discussions with the estate and had found them impossible to deal with. In fact, he claimed, they had specifically and in no uncertain terms flatly rejected negotiating for a purchase of the tapes. Their position seemed to be that pretty much anything and everything having to do with Jimi was *already* their property. Indeed, more than one source had informed me that the estate's attorneys were beginning to aggressively stake out a position that any such material was, in effect, "stolen property."

The situation before me was rather stark: (A) The owner of the tapes was intent on selling them one way or another, and (B) there was no way he was going to deal with the estate. EMP's choice was to take a chance on acquiring them or, possibly, to see the tapes disappear in the black hole of collectordom.

Perfectly intrigued, I flew to London in March 1998 to review the tapes at CTS Recording Studios, where I would attempt to determine their authenticity, physical condition, and musical quality. Impressed by the immaculate condition of the tapes—their container boxes even bore some handwriting by Jimi, whose unique penmanship is easily recognizable—I was floored by the music. The seller's agent and the studio's staff engineer patiently indulged me by cueing up and playing whatever portions of any of the tapes I asked to hear.

The entire session was, for this longtime Hendrix aficionado, an unforgettable once-in-a-lifetime chance to hear rock 'n' roll music that few, if any, other ears had heard in almost three decades. It was a magic moment. I felt like an audio version of an archaeologist who happened upon a cave opening, crawled in, and came face-to-face with undiscovered examples of awesome rock art that had been left by long-dead masters of the form. Listening to these tapes in the acoustic environment of a top London studio added to the experience. In time, I became convinced of the tapes' authenticity and high quality, and returned home with a glowing report.

Though EMP couldn't know exactly how we'd ever use the tapes at the museum, we did think that these long-missing tapes, now suddenly surfaced, might slip away forever if we didn't act to safeguard them. So, within forty-eight hours, I flew back to London and cut the deal. I was elated, if somewhat jet-lagged, and once our collections crew arranged to have the tapes shipped (they were flown back in lead-lined crates) and safely stowed in the security vault, our publicity team decided to crow a little bit.

A press release was issued announcing this prominent acquisition, and I found myself doing interviews about it with reporters from all over the world. Numerous international news outlets quoted me as saying things along the lines of "These rare recordings are true works of art. They are long-lost reminders of an electric guitar master at his absolute peak . . . These recordings are the missing link. They are the aural evidence that music fans and scholars have needed in order to allow further study of the development and evolution of Hendrix's skill and artistic style . . . Having heard the tapes now, I can assure you that additional proof of his genius comes through loud and clear."

Even if future scholars would one day be thrilled that we'd salvaged the tapes from an unknown fate, other people were apparently pissed off. It eventually came to my attention from an inside source—my new telephone pal and Jimi's former bassist, Noel Redding—that certain members of the Hendrix estate were irked about all the clamor that this acquisition was sparking in the media. They were particularly angry—or so I heard—at *me*. Talk about wanting to kill the messenger! So, no more Hendrix estate party invites for me . . .

And this, even though when asked by reporters about EMP's plans for the tapes, I'd responded forthrightly that "we do not have any plans to release them commercially, but we are exploring the many ways that they can be integrated into the museum—exhibits, education, etc.—so that EMP can preserve and protect the tapes, but at the same time allow museum visitors to learn from and experience this amazing part of Hendrix's career."

Well aware that Al Hendrix had been unjustly robbed of income from Jimi's royalties (not to mention the intellectual property rights) two decades prior, I had no desire whatsoever to aggravate the estate over this tape matter. Indeed, I felt nothing but gratitude to Al for having been so generous to me with his time over the years, and I truly wished him all the luck in the world in his battle to reclaim those rights.

So I was extremely happy for him when, on July 28, 1995, the $5 million sum that Paul Allen reportedly loaned the estate helped result in a total legal victory—one that returned those hugely profitable intellectual property rights to the estate. At long last, Jimi's family saw justice and their hardest years of struggle were in the past. And so, apparently, were any possible hard feelings between the estate and EMP: the next time I crossed paths with Al (in the Hendrix Gallery at EMP's grand opening) he took a moment to shake my hand, smile his twinkly-eyed smile, and personally thank me for all my efforts.

▶ The peghead from a rare 1930s Seattle-made Audiovox electric guitar.

GUITAR MANIA

"MILLION-DOLLAR" GUITARS?

One major downside to buying anything at highly publicized auctions is that the details of who bought what often become known. I can't prove that the auction houses themselves betray confidentiality agreements with their bidders, but it sure seems that leaks are not uncommon.

Goodness knows that after Hendrix's famous white Fender Woodstock Stratocaster sold at public auction back in 1991—and at $325,000 set a world-record price for a publicly sold electric guitar—word eventually spread that Paul Allen had acquired it. Once the cat was out of the bag, you could tell word got around: "Hey! That billionaire guy in Seattle is starting a rock 'n' roll museum and they're buying up tons of stuff!" Similarly, once we revealed—through our 1996–97 Strats, Studios, and the Seattle Sound exhibit—that we'd acquired a major shard of the Stratocaster that Hendrix had so famously burned and smashed onstage at the Monterey Pop Festival in June 1967, my phone rang off the hook with offers to sell the remaining missing portions of that guitar. There was simply no end to the flood of solicitations from supposed artifact holders.

My job entailed taking all offers seriously until I determined they were not worthy of further consideration. In the case of the Monterey Stratocaster, anyone who's seen the full-length motion picture of the Monterey concert (and is able to count) can see that Hendrix clearly sets the guitar on fire with lighter fluid, smashes it all to hell on the stage floor, and then, once the poor instrument is shattered beyond playability (or repair), proceeds to toss four sizable chunks of it into the stoned and stunned audience. My own curiosity about the possible whereabouts of the guitar's unaccounted-for remains got the better of me once, and I was quoted in the *Seattle Times* pondering the mystery: "The scary thing is, Jimi is clearly shown in the video throwing four pieces of that guitar to four separate people.

Where are those other three pieces? Someone may still have the neck from that guitar!"

Simply by uttering that inquiry, I instantly learned to never ask a question you don't want an answer to. In short order I heard from at least three sources, all trying to sell—for a certain price—what they claimed were those long-missing pieces.

One guy called me stating that he wanted to sell a chunk of the Monterey guitar. *Great! I'm all ears*. . . Surprisingly, the initial story of provenance sounded reasonably good; at least I saw no obvious factual errors that would instantly rule out the thing's authenticity. As I recall, he claimed to have attended the Monterey show himself and had carefully held onto the wooden guitar chunk all these years. In truth, my mind was already racing ahead, thinking about how fun it would be to get a photograph of the thing and see at least whether it had any hope of matching up with the shard EMP already had. But the seller's mind was jumping ahead as well: not only was a request for a photo instantly denied, but the voice on the other end of the line had the nerve to skip all sorts of steps in this dance and blurt out those dreaded deal-killing syllables: "And I wanna get $1 million for it." End of story.

"Wanting" and "getting" are, of course, worlds apart. It seemed as if everybody was getting starry-eyed about Allen's money, without ever pausing to review the facts: no guitar in history had ever sold for $1 million. Not the prime shard of the Monterey guitar that we already had, not even the whole, complete Woodstock guitar. Rationality dictated that other wooden slivers must be worth some lower amount. Ah, yes, but that formulation invoked the concept of reason—a trait that seemed to be in an ever decreasing supply.

Conversely, the supply of offers kept ringing on in. There was, for instance, the caller who wanted to sell the burnt guts—or rather, the electronic pickups, wires, potentiometers, knobs, and pickguard—that had fallen from the Monterey guitar's body cavity upon its fiery destruction. Well now, *this* was certainly an interesting one. In fact,

I don't think I'd ever even stopped to ponder the whereabouts of those particular portions of the famous instrument. EMP surely didn't have them. The man who'd tried to sell what he'd purported to be the other missing main body shard didn't have them. So, sure, this possibility was at least somewhat intriguing. But just as Fender necks are interchangeable, every Stratocaster ever made also had a set of essentially interchangeable guts.

The seller consented to send photographs, a positive step. But upon the images' arrival, the first problem became apparent: all I could make out in the photos was an ugly, undifferentiated gnarled black mess of molten plastic and copper wires. And the whole seemed to be displayed in some kind of deluxe shrinelike, glass-enclosed, oak-framed box, replete with, I think, built-in lighting. The only things missing from this overblown tableaux were the Rockettes, a laser show, and clouds of dry-ice smoke.

Nevertheless, and with considerable reluctance, I followed up with a phone call to discuss the matter further. Mercifully, it was a quite brief discussion because I'd swear I heard a certain dollar figure mentioned—a figure that, due to the nature of its extreme absurdity, I'll refrain from even mentioning here. Suffice it to say, things were truly starting to get wacky. But the wackiness hadn't yet peaked, as I'd soon find out.

Another afternoon, another phone call. This time it was a seller claiming to have the Monterey guitar's neck. Although in the back of my mind I thought, "This is getting to be like the ten thousand slivers of the one true cross of Jesus," a sense of professional duty prevailed upon me to follow through. So began the game of Twenty Questions: "Thanks for calling in. I'd love to know every last thing you can tell me about how you came into ownership of the item. How long have you had it? Were you at the concert?" And so forth . . .

As I recall and paraphrase here, the response was, "Uh, well, no. You see, I got it from a friend whose now-deceased father had dated a girl back in the Summer of Love, and he said she said that blah, blah,

blah . . . so we're pretty sure that this thing we just found in the base-ment is the same one that he said she said was the one that . . . "

Yikes! This kind of trail of ownership was woefully and comi-cally inadequate, but I did go so far as to indulge in a request for a photograph—and when that actually arrived I could see that it defi-nitely was indeed a Stratocaster neck. Problem is, there have only been about a gazillion of those made since 1954 (albeit with slight design variations over the years). But just then the phone rang again and here was our seller chomping at the bit, wondering if we were ready to buy it yet.

I calmly tried to slow him down, pointing out the hurdles of proof we still faced, and how I'd like to work with him to establish more reasons why EMP should be convinced that it was the cor-rect neck. What did this offer of cooperation get back in return? A brusque suggestion that it was I who needed to prove the thing wasn't authentic—and that the price to buy it would be, of course: "$1 million."

Without one solid shred of evidence backing it, I would never have tried to run such a weak proposal up the flagpole at EMP. Maybe it *was* the right neck, but when a potential seller suggests that I should try and track down determinative information about *his* object—an object he isn't willing to deliver for further scrutiny—my interest necessarily evaporates. The time had finally arrived to set somebody straight about marketplace values. At lecture's end, our seller gave no ground, insisting that it was I who was being an impediment to his ability to reach Paul Allen.

My response was direct: "Sir, if you believe that, grab a pen. I'm going to give you the phone number to Paul Allen's personal assis-tant. I encourage you to give it your best shot there. And good luck." Because I never heard back about this matter—from either Allen, his executive assistant, or the seller—it's safe to assume that the deal dead-ended in an appropriate way.

In fairness, I should add that the distinct possibility does exist that all of those particular deals were perfectly legitimate offerings. It's just that each of these sellers way out of line, marketwise, in seeking such outrageous sales figures—especially when none of them had any documented proof of their item's authenticity.

As all this haggling over purported parts of the Monterey guitar continued, a new nuisance developed. Opening up a European publication one day, I came upon a disturbing assertion that our museum's Woodstock guitar was not the correct one. This wild—and unsubstantiated—claim led to an immediate forensics investigation, during which Jim Fricke and I analyzed the guitar in painstaking detail. Rest assured, after careful study of it against digitalized close-up still shots from the *Woodstock* film, we established that the unique light maple wood-grain pattern (a wooden neck's fingerprint of sorts) matched perfectly. Furthermore, the white enameled body bore all of the particular and unique nicks and dings apparent at the time Hendrix was playing it (along with a few additional ones, presumably gained in the years after Jimi gave it as a gift to his drummer, Mitch Mitchell). The evidence we noted was bulletproof, its provenance was impeccably documented, and it only remained a mystery why anyone would want to fabricate a malicious story about the guitar being inauthentic.

In none of those sales-offer instances did I mind the work at hand. It was always great fun to be approached by a seller, listen to the pitch, and then set about evaluating the plausibility of the claims. In some weird way, I often didn't care what the end result was—I just grew to enjoy hearing the spiel.

I can't begin to relate the number of other so-called Jimi Hendrix guitars that were offered up—but I do recall the one in Europe that would have required us flying the seller (and his girlfriend) to Seattle just to discuss a potential deal. Then there were the offers that originated from Seattle, like the instrument shown me by a supposed boyhood friend of Jimi's. Over the phone, he claimed it was Jimi's guitar back in the 1950s. But while meeting up in person, his story veered off-message and he proceeded, under my cross-examination, to 'fess up that, well, it was actually his own boyhood guitar—but that as Jimi's old jammin' buddy, he'd loaned it to him on a few occasions. Close, but no cigar. Another time, a certain local musician claimed to have a Stratocaster he insisted he'd picked up after one of Hendrix's homecoming concerts at the Seattle Center Arena. This sounded feasible, but then the musician mentioned that it was the guitar Jimi had burned. And that little detail created a big problem, because the experts—and even a few people who'd attended those shows—all denied that Hendrix ever torched a guitar here.

Even beyond guitars, whenever something had anything to do with Hendrix, that nice round figure of $1 million seemed to pop up—a syndrome I began to refer to as the "Paul Allen Special." As time went on and our Hendrix collection grew ever more robust, our little staff at EMP had some discussions, the upshot of which I later shared with a reporter at *The Rocket*: "Our team here has come to the understanding that we're not completists. For example, on Hendrix, we do pass on things that don't add any particular value to the collection, and we don't cry if we miss something and another collector gets it. We've got the best Hendrix collection in the world, and we've got some of the crown jewels, but do we need every magazine from every country that ever had an article on Jimi? No, we don't. Do we need every newspaper clipping [about Hendrix] from every small town? No, we don't. There *are* people who collect that stuff, and God bless them . . . But we don't need everything here, and we don't buy everything for the highest price that anyone could ever think of." Especially all those $1 million electric guitars floating around out there.

GUITARS GALORE

Having developed the electric-guitar history portion of EMP's Strats, Studios and the Seattle Sound temporary exhibit back in 1996, I was tremendously excited by the prospect of expanding it dramatically for the large guitar gallery in the museum's new building. The earlier exhibit had showcased a mere dozen or so fine instruments and, while popular, had been a minimal version of what I figured the guitar exhibit could ultimately be. As we looked at plans for the guitar gallery space, I calculated that the instrument selection could be expanded from a dozen to fifty or more.

I rethought the guitar history story line and conjured a mental image of how a display might be laid out in a linear/chronological manner, allowing people to see at a glance how guitar (and amplifier) design had evolved: from the first commercially produced electric—the 1932 Rickenbacker "Fry Pan"—right up through the essential classics (a 1952 Gibson Les Paul, a 1954 Fender Stratocaster) and on to a number of the very latest, high-tech space-age guitars. I sought to develop an exhibit that would help visitors understand that the very shape, size, and materials used in any particular model actually affected the sounds, and therefore the music, that came out of it.

When pitched to the team, this comprehensive exhibit concept was met with high regard. The idea conformed perfectly to the original team's institutional goals of highlighting innovation in music, as well as an early exhibit goal we'd committed to years before: that of focusing on the tools used by creative musicians. Once given the green light, I drew up a timeline that charted every important innovation that I could document throughout guitar history—a timeline that was then easily converted into a prioritized shopping list of desirable specimens.

Now the really fun part began: tracking down museum-quality specimens and negotiating to acquire them at fair prices. I set out by soliciting the help of a few trusted friends in the guitar world, mainly knowledgeable collectors and enthusiasts, rather than deal-ers. No one ever saw my wish list, no one was told of the overall plan. And for a couple years that worked fine. I reeled in incredible instru-ments from all over the country. At all times, I attempted to stick to the script and grab only guitars already noted on the list, but when you dive into a topic, there are always more surprises and discoveries to be made. You might start out thinking that you just need examples of the main models that define this history, but sometimes the odd-ball, evolutionary dead-end models can help make a certain point.

This guitar-collection developmental process was labor inten-sive. For every guitar I acquired, there were scores of others that were considered and rejected. The collecting criteria demanded that each addition be in unmodified, all-original condition, as close to mint shape as possible. The problem was that in the world of guitars, every model I was searching for was already a high-demand item. As guitars worthy of the museum exhibition, they were also, by definition, fine instruments that plenty of other collectors (and players) were seeking. Hope of scoring fantastic bargains every time was not realistic.

With a couple years to go before turning over everything to an exhibit designer, I knew I probably had adequate time to accomplish the goal. Then again, this guitar exhibit was (along with the North-west and Hendrix exhibits) only one of the collections I was building simultaneously. It was a crazy and harried pace, but this was also one of the most exciting phases yet.

THE MISSOURI BREAK

With a deadline drumbeat pounding away in my brain, I began aggressively looking for ways to speed the collect-ing process along. On one particular adventure, I followed up on a lucky break that came my way. I'd received a lead about an

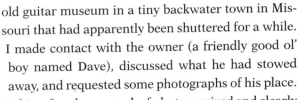

old guitar museum in a tiny backwater town in Missouri that had apparently been shuttered for a while. I made contact with the owner (a friendly good ol' boy named Dave), discussed what he had stowed away, and requested some photographs of his place. Within a few days a stack of photos arrived and clearly showed a dusty old room (or three) stacked to the roof with amazing stuff. Immediately apparent were racks and racks full of interesting guitars of just about every type imaginable—and some that weren't.

A few close-up shots got my heart racing. One showed a unique hollow-body Spanish-style electric guitar (labeled with a 1940s date of origin) that was constructed from translucent plastic. Dave also had a deep stash of more-standard, and therefore relevant, instruments—vintage guitars and amplifiers that gave me the opportunity to test him as to the values he placed on certain quantifiable items. When satisfied that he wasn't intent on busting my budget, I made arrangements to visit him and scope things out.

Dave picked me up at the airport and we rode his battered pickup into the dying Mayberry-like hamlet. He unchained the doors to what was probably a century-old red-brick building that faced a charming though underpopulated town square. Then began a tour through an amazing collection of vintage, and occasionally weird, guitars and amplifiers that he'd mothballed when his museum dream had fizzled out. I took some notes as we plowed through his holdings, and I checked into a crummy motel a few hours

▲ The unique and way-ahead-of-its-time custom electric guitar made circa 1947 for country musician Jack Rivers by the legendary Paul Bigsby.

later, soon ruing the fact that the town—which was in a liquor-free dry county—also had no restaurants open at that late hour.

The next morning, after an early and big breakfast, we reviewed the items I'd found to be of interest. I was most intent on acquiring the earliest electric guitars and amps he had—and boy did he ever have them! Just the sight of all those old 1930s Rickenbacker and National amps lined up in a row still causes goosebumps. In particular, I fell in love with what was perhaps the oldest electric-guitar amp ever marketed: a beautiful brown "alligator" skin–clad oblong unit, with an awesome maple-toned wooden grill plate (over the speaker opening) that was shaped into the word "Dobro." Already attracted to the piece, I was hooked for sure when Dave mentioned that it had been acquired years before, directly from a member of the Doperya family, who had founded that pioneering company in Los Angeles.

All told, I think I cherry-picked about sixteen fine pieces out of the collection and returned to Seattle with a real sense of accomplishment. I had knocked a number of items off the wish list, all in one fell swoop. But that was a unique situation. No other such time-saving opportunity ever arose again, and from there on out it would be one step, one guitar, and one amp at a time.

WISH-BOOK SHOPPING

Although raiding that Missouri guitar stash was a memorable and successful way of scooping up rare instruments for EMP's exhibits, far more typical were hunting trips that led to disappointment: often instruments weren't the correct models, or weren't in the condition described by a seller. Then there were the times that another buyer beat me to the punch and scooped something up before I could get to it. Oh well, all's fair . . .

The key was to remain calm and trust that all the essential items could be located in time. Given the slow pace at which these desired guitars and amps were turning up, I kept thinking about other ways to zero in on them. One day well into this amazing process, I was paging through some guitar collector–oriented magazine when my eyes landed on a photograph of an absolutely stunning one-of-a-kind freak electric guitar from 1947. It was so cool that the periodical had showcased it like a centerfold in *Playboy* magazine.

Granted, this was not a guitar that had been on my list. Nor was it an instrument that had had any perceptible influence on subsequent guitar designs. But, gawd! The physical characteristics of it alone spoke a thousand words about early efforts to electrify guitars. It was a combination of primitive design ideas and natural grace. It was just *beautiful*.

For a moment I was deeply disheartened. I thought, man, there really *are* some cool ultrararities out there that are missing from the history books. Important guitars that I'll never get my hands on for our exhibit. What a shame. This exhibit—the world's first comprehensive look at electric-guitar design and its impact on music—needs to be definitive, and here was a guitar we'd never be able to show. But as I sat there moping, it struck me: just because I haven't *yet* tried to persuade anybody to let loose of a guitar that they weren't already intent on selling doesn't mean I *can't* try!

With that ambition in mind, I brought the matter up with my supervisors. I don't know if they detected the urgency I felt about this guitar—and after all, it hadn't been on the original wish list because neither I nor probably anybody but its owner even knew the instrument existed—but they gave in to my wishes. I made a few calls, reached the owner, solicited a sales price that wasn't all that scary for a half-century-old instrument, and closed the deal. When the guitar eventually arrived, it was a glory to behold: a unique model of an exceedingly rare line of early electrics that had been handbuilt in California by Paul Bigsby—perhaps his first. And the bonus was: it had been custom-built for an old Seattle-based country star, Jack Rivers.

With that transaction, for the first time I realized the role I'd been charged with. If I could discover something—even while flipping through a "wish book," like someone longing for things in the old Sears, Roebuck catalog—and if I was able to justify its worth to the museum and strike a fair deal, odds were decent that my supervisors would back the effort. With that support, and a couple years to devote to the effort, I reeled in maybe sixty-five or seventy guitars (along with a good number of matching amps) and was well on the way to having all the instruments we'd need to mount a world-class exhibit.

THE GUITAR SUMMIT

The guitar exhibit was finally ready for a good testing in the summer of 1998. Knowing full well that I was no guitar expert, I thought it advisable to have a few recognized historians and experts vet my work before going much further. I invited such a group to what I called a Guitar Summit. This two-day meeting's tasks would be (1) to review the exhibit plans for accuracy and tone; (2) to examine about fifty-five vintage instruments and double-check their authenticity; and (3) to make certain that I'd not overlooked any critical guitar models that needed to be included.

The positive response to the invitation was gratifying, and those who responded included George Gruhn (author, dealer, and columnist for *Vintage Guitar* magazine), Richard R. Smith (author of definitive books on both the Rickenbacker and Fender guitar companies), John Teagle (historian and author), Jim Hilmar (collector and *Vintage Guitar* columnist), and Lynn Wheelwright (historian, luthier, and dealer).

We closely examined the guitar specimens that I was proposing to use in the exhibit, and new (at least to me!) details about their construction or other design attributes were pointed out. I think it's safe to say that the assembled were impressed not a little bit that I'd managed in just a few short years to acquire prime examples of these guitars—and first-year-of-issue examples at that. The ad hoc team also spent another full day reviewing and critiquing the exhibit outline as it existed, and numerous valuable additions, corrections, or suggestions for slightly different angles of "message emphasis" were contributed. As might have been expected from such a passionate group of guitar lovers, recommendations were made for the acquisition of a few substitute guitars. Believe you me, that advice was promptly followed up on over the next few months, with a lot of double-time hustling. But the best news was that at the summit's end, a great sense of accomplishment arose when the participants honored the overall exhibit plan with a big thumbs up. With that seal of approval, I knew the approaching deadline would be met and everything would be turned over to the exhibit designers on schedule.

▶ An unused 1965 promotional poster blank advertising a dance by the Kingsmen.

SHOW and DANCE

Featuring . . .

The . . .

KINGSMEN

. . . . . RECORDING STARS OF . . . . .

"Louie, Louie"   "Little Latin Lupe-Lu"

"Jolly Green Giant"   "Money"   "Do The Climb"

TILGHMAN PRESS, 1217 - 32nd ST., OAK. - 653-4380

THE NORTHWEST CHALLENGE

Though each EMP exhibit—the Hendrix Gallery, the guitar gallery, and the Northwest gallery—posed its own unique challenges, it was the Northwest gallery that seemed most fraught with land mines.

First, both the Hendrix and guitar exhibits would be based significantly on stories supported by established history. Conversely, the Northwest gallery—or at least the grunge-era portions—would attempt to boil down a lot of recent history in some coherent and meaningful fashion. The Northwest exhibits would necessarily be based on my interpretation of various events—events that had taken place locally; events that had involved lots of people and bands that were still alive and well; events that were still fresh memories in a lot of people's minds.

Perhaps these issues should have bothered me more—they certainly were terrifying a number of the inexperienced junior members we'd recently added to our Curatorial Department—but I was comfortable by now with my responsibility for developing the Northwest gallery. I'd closely watched the whole grunge thing unfold. I knew many of the key players who'd ridden the juggernaut to international fame. And—as with each of the other exhibits I was developing—I fully intended on vetting the eventual exhibit outline with a few other experts before committing to it. So I was perfectly game to lead our team onward into the swamps of local music politics.

And those swamps sure proved to be murky and full of quicksand. A main complicating factor concerned the particular, and peculiar, mindset among the tight-knit grunge-era bands. A key ethical position within the scene was a disdain for careerism—a dislike of anybody who displayed any sense of obvious concern for getting ahead, for becoming *rock stars*. In a magazine article that later touched on the challenges I faced, *The Rocket* succinctly nailed the situation this way: "Seattle. A city where the performers are not exactly renowned for enjoying the glare of the spotlight even in the best of times."

Unfortunately for me, the time period when I approached some of the most successful local bands in an effort to apprise them of our exhibit plans—and to seek their blessings and/or help—could in no way be considered as anything like "the best of times." The grunge movement had already peaked. Nirvana's Kurt Cobain had been dead for a couple years. Alice in Chains was effectively paralyzed due to singer Layne Staley's drug problems—problems that would soon lead to his death. And Pearl Jam had taken a very public stand against Paul Allen for his recent investment in Ticketmaster; it wasn't long before word passed along the grapevine that the band was quite cynical about our museum project. Working around such land mines seemed daunting. But I remained hopeful that the integrity of my exhibit plans would eventually win over some of the skeptics.

Around 1997 I bucked up and decided to face this challenge head-on. This required so much of my time that I delegated one of my favorite tasks to another team member, Jacob McMurray, EMP's first curatorial assistant. McMurray happily took over making the weekly rounds of local record shops to pick up all those freebie posters and handbills and also to buy any newly released local records or CDs. In fact, he expanded the network to additional stores, and a result McMurray's knowledge about posters and Northwest music grew, and a half-dozen years later he went on to earn a position as a fine curator for the museum.

Meanwhile, I forged ahead and began making contact with the musicians (or their managers). True to form, some of these people were cynical and suspicious about EMP and its goals when first approached. That a software titan was behind this effort to bottle up and market a presentation of their own accomplishments and history was unnerving for some of them.

I believe that my sincerity, knowledge of the subject, and reputation usually convinced these musicians that it was at least worthwhile to meet up and hear me out. And by then I'd honed a pitch that seemed to work:

I think I understand why you may be skeptical. The thought of a museum trying to represent your contributions to music may be unappealing to you. Maybe you can't stand the idea of seeing your stage attire mounted on a mannequin in a glass display case. Maybe you aren't ready to see your art interpreted by a curator. Maybe you object to the very thought of a rock 'n' roll museum. That's okay. You don't know us, and we don't even have a museum building we can show you. I think I would be skeptical too. In point of fact, though, I'm a music fan first and a music curator second. I love the Northwest scene. I intend on representing it in as honest, fair, and interesting a manner as possible. I want the exhibits to be both engaging and representative of some truths. This will not be some lightweight Hall of Fame. We will not have grungy flannel shirts and Doc Martens boots mounted like taxidermy displays on mannequins. There will be edgy messages conveyed. I will not allow for any sanitizing or whitewashing of this history. So really, I'm with you: until the museum is actually up and running, I too will retain some of my skepticism. Now let me assure you of what I also know: Paul Allen has thus far been an excellent leader for this project. He is fully supportive of our plans for the galleries. He has the expectation that the eventual exhibits will meet the highest qualities, both physically and intellectually. And, lastly, please trust me when I tell you that neither Paul, nor anybody upstairs, has thus far made any moves whatsoever to meddle in any curatorial/content issues . . . So, do you think you might see your way to helping my efforts here?

I'm proud to say this kind of entreaty worked more often than not. With a very few, but notable, exceptions most everybody was willing to hear the pitch. Those who did generally loved the exhibit concepts, and many ended up graciously loaning or even donating serious artifacts for display.

Of the leading grunge bands, Mudhoney was among the first to respond favorably. Their guitarists, Mark Arm and Steve Turner, heard me out, admired my curatorial take on the Northwest story, and instantly threw in their support—which eventually included providing instruments (a grungy Fender guitar and the actual Univox Super-Fuzz and Electro Harmonix Big Muff stompbox distortion pedals they'd used, and even named their debut album after) as well as agreeing to do oral history interviews. Conversely, I struggled for a couple years to break through and get the attention of other acts or their management. My efforts at dialogue of any sort with the management of Soundgarden, Alice in Chains, and Pearl Jam were mostly all for naught.

It didn't help matters when some magazine published a report that EMP had recently paid good money for one of Eddie Vedder's old toothbrushes. While perfectly untrue, that kind of gossip must have created a sense that we were vultures looking to pick at whatever bones we could find. In actuality, I was discerning when it came to pondering the acquisition of questionable items. When offered some truly weird artifacts over the years—like Layne Staley's rancid Doc Martens, Kurt Cobain's medical prescription bottle, and even Jimi Hendrix's pot pipe—I easily passed on such "opportunities."

Through a back channel within the Pearl Jam camp, I heard that they simply didn't want to have *anything* to do with "Paul Allen's toy museum," as they termed it. And repeated invitations to review exhibit plans with Soundgarden or their management never were accepted. Over time, however, there were small victories on these fronts: Pearl Jam's amiable guitarist, Mike McCready, agreed to sit for one of our first oral history video interviews; Soundgarden's guitarist, Kim Thayil, eventually agreed to meet, and he ultimately donated his band's old 1986 Chevy touring van, along with providing a long-term loan of one of his signature guitars.

Meanwhile, Nirvana's bassist, Krist Novoselic, agreed to stop by my office and discuss the situation. Hearing my spiel, Novoselic (who arrived with a lawyer in tow, just to be sure) was noticeably pleased when he got the "right" answers after querying me about various exhibit aims and approaches. The happy result was that he became most helpful, agreeing to an oral history session and then loaning us numerous awesome artifacts. These included his famous black bass guitar (and *Nevermind*-era amp head), a set of rehearsal-space drums used by Dave Grohl, and even the winged-angel stage props from Nirvana's *In Utero* tour.

With this kind of material in addition to what we already had collected, the grunge exhibit was promising to be quite impressive. Consider: Back in July 1994 I answered a *Seattle Times* classified ad that read, "Nirvana collection for sale." I drove up to Oak Harbor, where I met with the sellers, who turned out to be the family of Nirvana's first drummer, Chad Channing. When the band had made their earliest tour to England and Europe, he'd been the one to mail back home concert posters and photos and obscure European press-ings of Nirvana's records. But his parents were crushed by Cobain's death in April 1994, and they wanted to be rid of anything that con-jured memories that were "too painful." This sad situation enabled the museum to acquire a prime stash of rare artifacts.

Then, over the next few years, we also reeled in gold and plati-num records marking Nirvana's various album sales, a set of twelve handwritten lyrics Cobain had penned in 1988—and Nirvana's orig-inal recording contract signed with Sub Pop Records, which was acquired from the band's second guitarist, Jason Everman, via auc-tion. In addition, I made it a priority to track down as many early Nirvana gig posters as possible. These were proven to be a valuable graphic record when, in 2004, the band's own label and management accessed EMP's archives, publishing images of many of those rare posters in their four-CD retrospective set, *With the Lights Out*.

But the most significant finds were the three Cobain guitars I acquired. The first was the sunburst Fender Stratocaster smashed in Florida and acquired via Guernsey's auction house; the second was hauled in from a local pawnshop; and the third one—a very recognizable Univox-brand instrument—was simply offered to us by a lucky young man from Olympia who'd picked it up off the floor after Cobain had shattered and abandoned it during an early Nirvana show at Evergreen State College in 1988.

The pawnshop guitar in particular was an interesting acquisition, as it occurred purely by chance. One evening during dinner I happened to be ignoring a local TV newscast when my ears perked up during a zany piece about the wide variety of things that filled the shelves of some little pawnshop located in Seattle's Capitol Hill neighborhood. What really triggered my attention was that the manager claimed to have a black Fender Stratocaster formerly owned by Kurt Cobain. I followed up the next day and the shop's owner confirmed the story, adding interesting details about how a certain troubled Seattle rock star had recently pawned the Cobain instrument while experiencing some financial difficulties. In fact, that famous singer, who'd been a close friend of Cobain's (and who'd received the instrument from him as a gift), had also pawned some of Cobain's shirts and other things—all of which constituted perfectly convincing evidence that the story was true. We negotiated and settled on a price—a price that museum ethics preclude me from divulging, but one that *Mojo* magazine quoted me as characterizing as not being a typical "pawnshop price."

COURTING LOVE

Even with all these gems locked away in EMP's vault, I figured that there were plenty of good reasons to try to directly win the support of Kurt Cobain's widow, Courtney Love. My goals in meeting with her were threefold: (1) I thought that she, of all people, deserved to know about the grunge exhibit; (2) I believed her input could be invaluable; and (3) I of course wouldn't have objected if she offered to loan additional materials for the display.

We met up one late afternoon at the Elysian Brewing Company on Capitol Hill. When she saw that I was legit and harmless, Love dismissed her escort/driver and we proceeded to have a very nice little lunch and get-acquainted session. I offered her an overview of EMP, my curatorial goals, and as much info as she wanted about the exhibits. She was charming, friendly, and seemingly pleased with

▲ The customized Univox Hi-Flyer electric guitar smashed onstage by Kurt Cobain at Nirvana's October 30, 1988 gig at Evergreen State College in Olympia.

what she was hearing from me, even going so far as to suggest a tour of her and Cobain's Leschi neighborhood home—the one where Cobain, sadly, had committed suicide. She wanted to show me some interesting items there, and so I drove her home in my Jeep.

Love graciously walked me through her home and then led me down to the basement, where she showed me stacks of her and Cobain's guitar cases and amplifiers; I even stole a quick peek at their records. *Damn*, it is so enjoyable to look through other people's collections, especially when I spy things like Sonics LPs among them! But what she really wanted me to see was Cobain's art room, which held a mess of stuff like broken doll parts, heart-shaped boxes, tree leaves, other strange found objects, and oil-painting supplies. I'd followed his story since the 1980s and so already knew that he'd long dabbled in painting. Indeed, probably the very first Northwest-related acquisition EMP had made was a very cool painting from Cobain's high-school days that featured a punked-out, mohawked, and black leather–clad post-apocalypse couple (à la Grant Wood's *American Gothic*) standing before the grim ruins of an imploded nuclear reactor. So I was more than happy to have a look. What she showed me was fascinating: a storage container that Cobain had kept his painting supplies in, namely a battered old guitar case.

I instantly reacted by exclaiming how absolutely cool that was. It was a perfect physical representation of Cobain's artistic nature and his uniqueness as a songwriter/painter. I let her know that if she ever wanted to see that displayed, EMP was the place. At the tour's end, I thanked her and we agreed to keep in touch. It was an agreement I soon came to regret.

Over the next few months I heard back several times from Love—well, not exactly directly from her, as she had assigned an assistant to interact with me. All these phone calls from the assistant were aimed toward one exceedingly strange goal. Love, I was informed, wondered if Paul Allen would be willing to intercede on her behalf with city leaders and find some way to create a downtown park memorializing Cobain.

I was taken aback and, amidst some stammering and stalling over this completely left-field suggestion, pointed out that the best approach might be to submit a more detailed and specific proposal to Allen's business analysts at Vulcan. That was how huge projects like the one being suggested got considered. I merely worked for the museum project, and a park idea was out of my area of responsibilities. Apparently, this response wasn't good enough. I soon heard back that Love was "counting on me" to try and shepherd her idea upstairs, that if I had hopes for any cooperation from her I'd definitely want to push this idea along.

Bribery is not to my liking, and I wasn't going to tolerate the implied threat of noncooperation. If Love wanted to have any input on the grunge exhibit, I told her, now was the time for her to offer help. I calmly explained that if a memorial park idea was ever to be considered, such a project would be on an entirely different time line.

Pushed again about the park, I pushed back, saying something like "Look, you need to understand: Seattle fans battled for *years* to get something to honor Jimi Hendrix. They too wanted something nice placed in a city park—and what did they get? A stupid rock at the zoo. The local powers that be opposed every decent proposal ever made. Now, maybe a push for a Cobain park would be an easier sell, and I wish you all the luck in the world. But I'm going to go out on a limb here and guess that Paul Allen already has his hands full trying to get all sorts of permits for EMP's construction approved by various city departments. He very well may want to help out—but you'd need to ask him."

This was not a satisfactory response, I came to learn. Love involved her New York–based publicist/manager, and suddenly my phone was ringing off the hook and various ugly faxes started rolling in. The messages essentially amounted to claims that I was a roadblock to her dreams for a park, a park that Love needed as a solution to a very real problem. It was explained to me, you see, that she had been refused a burial place for Cobain's remains by numerous local cemeteries who, having learned from the example of Hendrix's trampled gravesite, didn't need or want to host a dead rock star who would inevitably attract a circus of grieving disciples and souvenir hunters. That, I could see, *was* a genuine problem—but it wasn't Paul Allen's problem.

Again I calmly tried to explain by phone that my sense was that Allen would likely respond to her idea by noting that his current project—a museum dedicated to music—was his way of honoring Cobain's contributions to music. I explained that I was leading the development of the specific exhibit that would represent Cobain, and—if they recalled—that was why we had made contact in the first place.

No luck. Love's vision had calcified into a desire for a park—apparently to be financed by Allen—that would have fountains and trees and some sort of stone monument with a flowing water feature where she could finally inter Cobain's ashes. Love and her people had even, if I recall correctly, gone so far as to have an architect draw up sketches of this pipe dream.

By this point I should have been smart enough to resist further entanglement with Love's people—but I wasn't. Responding to a suggestion that the Cobain park could be located adjacent to the EMP building, I countered with a sincere suggestion that maybe Cobain's ashes could be placed in the cornerstone of the museum's foundation. The blowback came with hurricane force and was along the lines of "How *dare* you! How *rude*! If *you* were Courtney, would *you* want *that*?! What would *you* do with Kurt's ashes if *you* were Courtney?" Pissed off now, and foolishly taking the bait, I again responded honestly, "You're asking me what *I* would do? Well, I don't really know. But maybe it would be to take them down to some nice, beautiful, trickling stream flowing out of the Olympic Mountains near his hometown and quietly scatter them there."

Live and learn. In hindsight, the proper response to such a personalized and open-ended inquiry would have been to say *anything* other than what I had just blurted out. The withering attack I faced after making that well-meaning-if-naïve suggestion proved that I'll never have a successful career as a diplomatic funeral-home director. Love's tag-teaming pit bulls lambasted me over the phone with denunciations about how I'd just "disrespected" the memory of Kurt Cobain and how I was such a cad for erecting hurdles between Love and Paul Allen.

I was disheartened and sick. After all, I had been one of Nirvana's earliest fans and simply loved the band's music. I'd collected hundreds of artifacts documenting their career. I was, in case she'd forgotten, preparing to curate an exhibit that included the band in a respectful and prominent way. This nasty turn of events just *sucked*. And it especially sucked when Love went on the warpath against me, having her people fax very aggressive and unhelpful letters to just about anyone in a position senior to mine at EMP, to the director of the Seattle Center, and probably to the mayor and city council, for all I know.

Those efforts were all for naught, though. The exhibit planning went forward and the Cobain park never happened. Meanwhile, various notices have been posted on the Internet in the years hence stating that Love—whom the media has long reported as hauling poor Cobain's ashes around stuffed inside her teddy bear—has taken the step of interring at least some of them in a rather interesting place: the Wishkah River, which trickles out of the Olympic Mountains and flows into the bay at his old hometown of Aberdeen.

Maybe I should reconsider a possible future gig working at a funeral home after all . . .

▶ Elvis Presley's vintage black leather motorcycle jacket.

THE SCHOOL OF HARD ROCKS

While scouring the planet for rock 'n' roll artifacts, I began hearing murmurs of discontent from out in the field. Friendly dealers and collectors mentioned in passing that the curatorial staff at both the Hard Rock Cafe restaurant chain and Cleveland's Rock and Roll Hall of Fame and Museum were grumbling about how aggressively I was scooping up great music-related artifacts.

The resentments in each case were, I think, a bit different. The Hard Rock guys had been actively buying music memorabilia as décor for about twenty-five years, and they had become used to dominating the market without facing any real competition. I'm guessing that they just plain hated to see another serious buyer show up on what had been almost exclusively their turf.

I had long questioned the very premise of the Hard Rock empire—that of displaying rock 'n' roll rarities in close proximity to some overpriced burger joint's greasy kitchen. The proven popularity of these restaurants in no way excuses that physical arrangement. Just refer to the artifact-handling guidelines of the American Association of Museums. Hanging priceless artifacts over tables where tourists gorge themselves on hamburgers and french fries doesn't even begin to meet the minimal conservation standards required for membership in that organization of serious professionals and their various institutions.

In my travels for EMP I never knowingly crossed paths with any Hard Rock buyers, nor had I bumped into them at auctions or guitar shows. In fact, I hadn't any clue that I'd been frustrating them . . . except for hearing those whispered gripes about how it was EMP that was responsible for driving up prices. How anyone decided that we alone could be blamed for this escalating trend remains beyond me.

What I did know was that more and more reporters were lobbing questions about this perceived clash between our organizations, though not everybody found grounds to disapprove. According to the now-defunct Web site SoundsofSeattle.com, "The implications of gathering together this mega amount of memorabilia [have] surely been a factor in skyrocketing prices at auctions. It's also limiting just how much memorabilia is left to go around. Used to be that Hard Rock Café and Planet Hollywood were two major contenders when it came to putting an item on the block. Now with EMP the stakes are even higher . . . Personally I'd much rather see the good stuff in a place of learning like EMP than over my burger and fries at the Hard Rock in Tuscany. I firmly believe that these items will do more good in inspiring others within that sort of venue than at an eating establishment." This sort of testimony that museums, not hamburger franchises, remain the preferred repositories of pop-culture treasures bolstered my own similar thoughts and hardened my resolve to steer clear of any burger joint boasting rock 'n' roll artifacts on its walls.

Foremost among the music museums supplying proper homes for these artifacts was the Rock and Roll Hall of Fame in Cleveland. Try as we might to create a relationship of cooperation, I suppose that as EMP's public profile rose through increasing media coverage of our activities, our reputation as the new 800-pound gorilla of the collecting world also spread. And it apparently began to grate on the Hall of Fame's nerves.

It's understandable that the Hall of Fame staff might be getting just a little envious watching EMP dropping considerable money to build a world-class permanent collection while they—reportedly without any budget earmarked for acquisitions—were necessarily stuck relying on the loan or donation of artifacts for display. The high quality of the Hall of Fame's wonderful inaugural exhibits, mind you, didn't indicate that they'd operated under such restraining circumstances, but it's still easy to imagine that they felt a bit threatened by our broad collection-development goals.

Although as their peers, the absolute last thing we wanted to do was create any sore points between the two organizations, a few clues about their real thoughts began surfacing in the media. The Hall of Fame's education director, Bob Santelli, once described EMP's style of aggressive collecting to the *Boston Globe*, saying, "They went out with both guns blazing." And *Newsday* reported that vice president for curatorial affairs Jim Henke "ruefully" bemoaned that "they're out there actively buying, and I would imagine their pockets are bottomless."

Although I may have appeared to be a trigger-happy gunslinger, indiscriminately targeting anything that moved, that just wasn't true. First of all, EMP was actually being reasonably selective in our collection-development efforts. That the museum probably did not acquire a majority of the items ever offered to us—and still built such a massive collection so quickly—merely serves as testimony to the vast quantity of rock artifacts out there.

Still, facts are facts, and media people couldn't help but want to compare and contrast our two organizations. They knew what the Hall of Fame was, but they struggled to figure out what EMP would be. And in our own way, EMP wanted the world to see a difference between the two museums—we had, after all, consciously planned to make EMP as unique an experience as possible. At the same time, we didn't want to cast those differences in a way that would disparage our friends in Cleveland. But I guess our belief that EMP's concept was superior in some ways shone through anyway.

Our early planning team believed that the world had been saturated with media coverage of—and museum (and restaurant) tributes to—the biggies from the 1950s and '60s, like Elvis and the Beatles. Where other places were fixated on honoring music's greatest overachievers, we saw value in representing the story of some of music's underdogs. Instead of focusing on the glory of a few players' accomplishments, it seemed important to try and highlight the broader creative communities that comprise a regional music "scene." Indeed, we saw room for an institution with a curatorial bent that was consciously focused on documenting and explaining various minority-taste, subculture musical movements (e.g., early independent punks and rappers), rather than focusing on the same old major-label superstars. Beyond that, we didn't want to fall into the easy trap of catering strictly to the aging baby boomer, *Happy Days*, looking-in-the-rear-view-mirror generation. As a reporter for *Willamette Week* wrote, "So what exactly is EMP supposed to be? If all those whip-smart staffers make one thing crystal clear, it's that they don't want the Experience Music Project to be the Rock and Roll Hall of Fame, West Coast Division. Everyone is assiduously nice about the Rock and Roll Hall of Fame. Still, it's plain that, to a certain extent, they're defining themselves against that Claptonized shrine to classic rock."

Perhaps it was the *New York Times* that first nailed the key difference: "Cleveland has the legends. Seattle stresses the indies." But one other big difference was, as *Newsday* quoted me, "they [the Cleveland staff] are bound to this Hall of Fame thing, so they're always going to be looking to the past." By contrast, wrote *Newsday*, "Because of its digital gadgetry, EMP . . . smacks of the future."

Indeed, not only did EMP have a forward-leaning institutional philosophy, but Paul Allen's interest in new technologies would also have a huge impact on just about every aspect of the museum's building and exhibits.

COLLECTING AT THE SPEED OF SOUND

In 1997, that whirlwind of a year, my duties revolved around the development of exhibits for the Hendrix Gallery, the guitar gallery, and the Northwest gallery, but I also began gathering quality artifacts whose eventual display purpose I couldn't possibly know.

Because I was coming across great items that didn't fit in those three exhibits, yet still showed great promise for spicing up some future display, I acquired them on faith that we'd find a way to use them at a later date.

One stunning piece was what some poster experts believe may be the only surviving specimen of a blues poster that promoted Mamie Smith and her band's 1920 recording "Crazy Blues," a tune that has been widely credited as the first blues song ever recorded. That item was offered to us by my pal Taylor Bowie, a local antiquarian book dealer who purchased a large book collection in the Midwest and later found the poster tucked into one large tome. Bowie kindly applied an unreasonably low "buddy price" to the priceless poster, and it flew straight into EMP's vault.

I also acquired some items previously owned by Elvis Presley. Elvis items, in general, are not all that rare. In fact, over the years there have been numerous all-Elvis auctions where a few hundred objects were sold each time. EMP had no immediate plans for any kind of

▲ Rare 1920s promotional poster advertising new OKeh Records blues recordings by Mamie Smith and Her Jazz Hounds.

Elvis exhibit—that seemed more like Rock and Roll Hall of Fame territory—but when I was approached by a former friend and associate of the singer (and a guy who had a long and uncontested track record in marketing his collection of Elvis items), I was all ears. This fellow was finally preparing to sell off some of his better items. Still, not much impressed me. Until, that is, I laid eyes on one item whose value to EMP was instantly apparent: Elvis's old black leather motorcycle jacket! In the blink of an eye I conjured a mental image of this artifact anchoring an exhibit that could survey the iconic usage of such jackets from Elvis through the Beatles, Sid Vicious, the Clash, Crass, and Darby Crash. Maybe, for yuks, it could even include Sha Na Na. Yes, an exhibit titled something like "Black Leather: The First 50 Years of Rockin' in Style." And so, after quickly doing my research and tracking down the handful of photographs I'd previously noted of Elvis wearing a couple different such jackets, I compared them, saw that one perfectly matched the jacket being offered, and cut the deal. I still hope to see that exhibit one day.

The major auction houses continued to provide us with opportunities for acquiring other prime artifacts, and that's where I successfully bid to acquire memorable things like Janis Joplin's paisley bell-bottoms, "flower power" blouse, pink feather boa, and funky love beads; some handwritten Doors lyrics by Jim Morrison; and Eric Clapton's famous red Cream-era cowboy shirt.

While our team gazed into the crystal ball to imagine what future shows we might want to mount, there was much enthusiasm for eventually doing a show dedicated to the blues. Following up on this, I made a trip to the heartland of the blues, the Mississippi delta. While I was in Clarksdale, a friend of a friend who was quite knowledgeable about local history provided an intriguing tour that included a look at the fabled crossroads where, back in the 1930s, blues legend Robert Johnson purportedly met up with the devil (and sold his soul in exchange for unprecedented guitar-playing skills).

I also toured places in Memphis like Sun Studios, where Elvis, Johnny Cash, Carl Perkins, Jerry Lee Lewis, Roy Orbison, and many other local hillbilly cats had cut their revolutionary rockabilly records back in the 1950s—and also where blues icons including Howlin' Wolf and B. B. King had early sessions. While in town I reviewed the exhibits at the brand-new Rock and Soul Museum and met up with the leaders of a planned Stax Museum to discuss their goals and explore any areas of common ground.

The main reason for the trip, though, was to check out the shuttered Memphis Music Museum, an odd and rather shabby private affair that had been founded years before by a local businessman and had reportedly struggled to find a role in the community. The museum was located just down the street from the fabled Peabody Hotel where I stayed, and after touring through the place while taking notes, I negotiated for the acquisition of a number of very hip items, including a couple of acetate discs cut at Sun Studios in 1952 by Howlin' Wolf, along with one of his trademark white suit coats, his old Fender amp (replete with his name handpainted in large white letters on top), and one of his harmonicas.

At some point, EMP's PR department got into the spirit of things and began to promote various acquisitions as they came rolling in, and all this activity began to capture people's imaginations. Reporters naturally wanted to talk about the nature of this high-end collecting. One journalist actually applied a certain, and not inaccurate, phrase—"dream job"—to my vocation well before I ever had. In an online entertainment Web site article titled, "A Piece of Rock: Buying Up Music's History—Now Here's a Guy with a Dream Job," she noted that, as a curator at EMP, I spend my time "quietly acquiring cool rock and roll trinkets ('artifacts,' in the museum biz), from specific instruments that pioneered new musical technologies to print materials—posters, press kits and private letters sent home by rock and rolling sons and daughters. The job's downside? Blecha doesn't get to keep these goodies. But then neither does museum bankroller and part-time rocker Paul Allen, from whom, Blecha jokes, he has had to retrieve, gently, more than one choice Stratocaster. He does get to write about the items and their significance to music history."

Another reporter took things even further by romanticizing my role in a very flattering way. In "Collection Agent: EMP's Very Own Indiana Jones," published in *The Rocket*, he wrote about my long track record: "Blecha is familiar to longtime denizens of Seattle's music scene . . . [H]e founded the Northwest Music Archives in the early 1980s, taking it upon himself to preserve and chronicle the region's rock and roll history . . . [P]eople came to regard Blecha as the repository for information and mementos relating to the region's musical chronology. That was then. Now, Blecha is one of the helmsmen of a multimillion-dollar venture that will transform Seattle's musical identity forever. As a senior curator for EMP's sizable collection of rock music's super-flotsam and mondo-jetsam, he's able to pick and choose what is purchased and exhibited. Truly, Blecha's avocation has been transformed into his vocation, and he wheels and deals in a deep-pocketed realm where no rock and roll collector has gone before!"

With these kind words and with the deadline drumbeat pounding ever louder in 1999, I kept on going. Even with at least eighty thousand artifacts already in EMP's collection, there was *much* more collecting still to do.

GUITARS OF THE STARS

As EMP's grand opening in 2000 loomed, so too did a few niggling concerns that while our planned exhibits were built on solid concepts, at least some of our expected visitors might be disappointed because we hadn't allotted much display space to the sure-fire, crowd-pleasing superstars of rockdom. By focusing on topics like Northwest regional music history, the story of the electric guitar, and the rise of punk rock and hip-hop, maybe we'd erred a bit by excluding blue-chip hit makers like the Beatles, Elvis, Dylan, and even Eric Clapton.

It was an unavoidable fact that entities like the Hard Rock Cafe had largely built their success on milking the general public's love for celebrity and fame, as opposed to presenting serious history. There was just no denying that—even though I had developed an acute aversion to the things— millions of average people got a significant thrill out of staring at guitars autographed by a well-known musical star.

Indeed, sales of such instruments—which I began to disparagingly call "star's guitars"—were growing by leaps and bounds. Almost every major (or minor) pop-culture auction during the previous decade had offered at least a few of them. The issue for me was that most of these instruments had never actually been owned, or even *played*, by the signatory artist. The damn things really existed only because a growing number of opportunistic autograph hustlers discovered that they could make a full-time living by dragging a knapsack full of blank electric-guitar pick guards around to get signed at the backstage doors of various concert arenas.

Jimi Hendrix's circa-1890 Washburn Type 9 acoustic guitar.

The best reason for despising this scandalous racket is that having a guitar inscribed with ink is unnatural, a form of defacement. But beyond that conservation/preservation matter is this important issue: getting a guitar signed by an artist is vastly different than acquiring a significant instrument that the same artist has used to create some great music. And having an artist sign just any model/brand of guitar, rather than the particular one that is widely associated with that musician, seems perfectly meaningless. Consider such screwball items as guitars signed by Ringo Starr and drumheads signed by Paul McCartney. To me such items make about as much sense as a football signed by Babe Ruth. What exactly is the point?

The main theme of my guitar history exhibit, on the other hand, was that these instruments had been selected specifically for their ability to represent milestones in the advancement of technological and/or design evolution. Furthermore, the music itself was affected positively because of those changes. For this display it wasn't important that we be able to assert that any particular instrument had been actually owned or played by a particular artist. Quite the contrary: each guitar was historically significant

▲ Hank Williams Sr.'s 1951 Gibson Southerner Jumbo acoustic guitar.

precisely because we could name numerous well-known artists who used that model of guitar to create their own signature sounds.

That said, while hunting down the last few instruments that the exhibit required, I couldn't rule out taking a look at the occasional guitar that had actually been owned or played by some big-name musician. In truth, there was no reason not to have such artifacts in our exhibits if they legitimately fit into the displays. On the rare occasions when the opportunity to acquire such guitars arose, I did just that. Throughout my eight and a half years at EMP I was lucky to acquire such instruments as Hank Williams Sr.'s 1951 Gibson Southerner Jumbo; Bonnie Guitar's 1951 Martin; Chuck Berry's 1973 Gibson ES-355TD; three of Jimi Hendrix's guitars (the black 1955 Gibson Les Paul that he played around 1962, his 1968 Martin acoustic, and his 1897 Washburn Type 9 acoustic that *Life* magazine included in a memorable October 3, 1969, photo spread); a 1956 Fender Telecaster formerly owned and played by Dave Davies of the Kinks; two of Billy "Hey Joe" Roberts's acoustic guitars; the 1964 electric Rickenbacker 360-12 Deluxe owned by Roger McGuinn that is heard on such folk-rock masterpieces as the Byrds' "Turn, Turn, Turn," "Mr. Tambourine Man," and "Eight Miles High"; two of KISS's over-the-top stage-prop guitars (Gene Simmons's Bloody Axe and Ace Frehley's Sparkle Star); and even one of Eddie Van Halen's customized Kramer guitars that helped rev up the heavy metal movement of the late 1970s and '80s.

BRINGIN' IT ALL BACK HOME

One of the more thrilling legendary instruments that I acquired for EMP was Bob Dylan's 1949 Martin 00-17 acoustic guitar. This particular instrument truly embodied some great history: It's the guitar young Robert Zimmerman used when he began developing his alter ego, Bob Dylan, by performing in folkie coffee houses around Minnesota back in 1959. And it's the same guitar that he'd used up through his arrival in New York City, including at his famous debut at Gerde's Folk City in Greenwich Village.

With this guitar, Dylan launched his near-mythic presence on a folk scene that he would soon rule. But perhaps most intriguing is that Dylan had taken the guitar to Woody Guthrie's bedside to play a few original songs for his sick and dying hero. Then, upon scoring a recording contract with Columbia Records in 1961—a deal that resulted in a debut album featuring songs like "Song to Woody" and "Talking New York," which must have been written on this very instrument—Dylan reportedly celebrated his newfound success by buying a new guitar and presenting this old Martin as a gift to the family that had kindly sheltered him when he'd been broke and struggling.

In their hands it rested all these years until they made the decision to part with it, placing the guitar with Christie's and thus opening the door for EMP and me to bring the historic piece out to Seattle. Our team immediately began planning an exhibit about Dylan's music that would be nicely anchored by this remarkable artifact.

▲ Bob Dylan's first acoustic guitar, the trusty old 1949 Martin 00-17.

LOST BUT NOT FORGOTTEN

Another instrument with an interesting story behind its discovery and authentication was a 1928 National guitar previously owned, played, and used in recordings by the early king of Chicago blues, Tampa Red. This instrument was originally discovered by the operator of a small-time Illinois-based guitar shop. To fully appreciate the tale, it should be noted that the whereabouts of most of the old instruments used by many early twentieth-century blues pioneers are unknown. So, for example, while Big Bill Broonzy's Gibson Style O guitar is accounted for (in a private collection), Robert Johnson's Gibson L-1 seems hopelessly lost. So too was the guitar pictured in old photographs of Tampa Red. The only real hope that it might ever turn up—and then be identifiable—came from the unique engraving pattern on the guitar's face, visible in the photos.

Then word bubbled up from a Texas guitar show that some guy had been going around from booth to booth with a 1928 National guitar claiming that it was Tampa Red's old instrument. What I first heard was that a few experts gave it a look and concurred: its design details did check out. It was, in fact, an authentic 1928 guitar. But beyond the stylistic features that helped peg its age, the damn thing also had that etching on the front: an *aged* etching that clearly spelled out these two words: Tampa Red.

Unfortunately, the guitar's owner drifted off into the crowds, and my sources didn't know if he'd ever found a buyer or not. So there was nothing I could do about it until my phone rang one day, and on the other end was this mysterious guitar-shop guy who claimed to have it and wanted to sell.

I slowed him down long enough to get a recap of his story. Given the obvious provenance issues, I needed to learn everything I could from him about the piece. And so the story unfolded: He'd received

▶ Bluesman Tampa Red's lost-and-found 1928 National Style 4 Tri-Cone resonator guitar.

a call one day from a little old lady in Aurora, Illinois, who wondered if his shop would want to buy her late husband's "old guitars." Once he was over at her house, the widow explained to him that her husband had been a musician many years ago and had even been involved in some recording sessions held downtown at the Leland Hotel's ballroom. Well, long story short, this dealer bought the guitars, returned to his shop, and was flabbergasted when he took a second look at the National and saw that distinct etching.

He was enough of a blues fan to know that Tampa Red had been based in Chicago, a mere 45 miles due east. So he was satisfied that he'd stumbled onto the real deal. I, however, needed to take the research process a number of steps further. But I also didn't tip my hand while I coaxed information out of the seller. For example, I didn't let on that the label that Tampa Red had recorded for, Bluebird Records, had, in fact, conducted a number of important recording sessions right there in Aurora. Furthermore, Tampa Red—and his early peers, including Big Bill Broonzy, Walter Davis, Yank Rachell, Speckled Red, Washboard Sam, Big Joe Williams, and John Lee "Sonny Boy" Williamson—had all cut seminal records in the sixteenth-floor ballroom of the Leland Hotel building. Interestingly, all this action stopped abruptly in 1940 when Bluebird's parent company, RCA Victor, built their own studios in Chicago. So at least the geographic details and information provided by the widow did not clash at all.

Next step? Photographic analysis. It took some real sleuthing, but by checking in with nationally recognized blues scholars and a few hard-core collectors, I was finally able to turn up a rare vintage image of Tampa Red and his guitar that far surpassed the quality of the rough image our seller had been able to provide. By comparing this to a photo of the guitar at hand, I ever so slowly became convinced: the finely wrought engraving of Tampa Red's name, and the intricate design flourishes surrounding it, were simply unique. They perfectly matched the guitar I was being offered.

Given the trouble I had in locating that corroborative photograph, I was confident that no one else could have done the same research and then also had the engraving skills to counterfeit Tampa's name onto a 1928 National. It's possible, I suppose, but why do it? I mean, Tampa Red is cool, but he's no Hendrix on the collectors' market. And when our seller mentioned a sizable—but still reasonable—asking price, it proved to me that he wasn't some kind of flim-flam man looking to retire early by selling it at a "Paul Allen Special" price.

GUITAR FEVER

After we decided on an actual grand opening date of June 2000, deadlines for EMP's various exhibits began to hit. The last and final exhibit gallery to be developed would present a number of iconic artists whose music represented a modern advancement of older music forms like folk and blues.

This Crossroads gallery is where the Dylan guitar and the Janis Joplin materials we'd gathered would be displayed. But there was still more space for another artist or two, and so I kept my eyes peeled for anything that might merit inclusion. That's about when the eye-popping spring 1999 catalog from Christie's arrived in the mail. As it turned out, this catalog represented a literal garage sale by one of the rock world's most revered guitar players ever, Eric Clapton. The mailing's sales pitch explained that he had culled the 105 listed guitars from his vast collection—and suddenly EMP was faced with a stunning opportunity, as well as a formidable series of challenges.

The international media had a field day: TV news and countless advance print features were broadcast and published for several weeks leading up to the auction. As usual, I scoured the catalog, noted which items EMP might best use, and quickly narrowed the options to just two individual guitars that were of serious interest. Many if not most of the guitars being offered were quite decent instruments, but very few could boast historical pedigrees. There were no claims, for instance, that these 103 other guitars were, say, "Clapton's longtime favorite," or a guitar that "Clapton played with his early groups, the Yardbirds, Cream, and Blind Faith," nor that "This guitar traveled the world on many successful concert tours." No, indeed. The less-interesting 103 guitars were what they were touted as: guitars from Eric Clapton's collection. Some he may have bought and conceivably rarely played. Some he'd received as gifts—and perhaps never played. And so forth.

But there were two extremely special guitars listed. Lot 98 consisted of a 1956 Fender Stratocaster that Clapton had toured with, and there was likely to be no shortage of documentary images (and/or film) of him performing with it. So that one could anchor a very satisfying exhibit. There was also Lot 105. This was the one that was getting all the attention in the guitar world, for it was none other than Clapton's famously favorite "Brownie"—the 1956 Stratocaster nicknamed by him for its "tobacco-burst" exterior finish. This was *the* guitar most associated with the guitar master. It was even featured prominently on two of his different album jackets from 1970: *Eric Clapton* and *Layla & Other Assorted Love Songs*. More importantly, it was the actual guitar he'd used to record those LPs, the latter of which has long been considered his finest work ever. That this Strat was the very one heard on the song "Layla"—easily one of the best songs issued that year and one of the finest guitar hook–ridden rock anthems ever preserved on a recording—made it the supreme star of the auction event.

I presented this information to Paul and Jody, and we all seemed interested in trying to acquire at least one of these Fenders. We discussed our game plan at length and agreed on some reasonable upper bid limits. But the question really was, what was reasonable? The estimated prices for the two guitars were, respectively, around $20,000–$30,000 and $80,000–$100,000.

I pointed out that while we agreed that Brownie was our priority—as it undoubtedly would be for various other bidders—it was also the final lot of the day. If we were outbid at that point we would probably regret that we didn't have a backup plan. Maybe we needed a Plan B. Perhaps we should sincerely try for Lot 98 (again, up to a reasonable level). Then we would still try and get Brownie. This felt a little extravagant, but I assured everyone that even if we ended up with both Clapton guitars, we could always use Lot 98 in the guitar gallery or perhaps loan it to our friends over at the Rock and Roll Hall of Fame. We all pondered this plan through those final days leading up to the big auction day of June 24, 1999. As best as I can now recall the exact circumstances, the Curatorial Department's new director, Chris Bruce, had probably been on board for only a couple weeks when the Christie's auction came up. And so, for fun, it was decided that Bruce would hang out at my desk and we'd share the excitement together when the bidding hour finally approached.

On auction day, phoned reports came in from a scout who attended in person. After Lots 1 through 10 had sold, the word was not good: even though those first guitars were relatively unremarkable, they'd still gone for roughly *four times* the posted pre-auction estimates. The bidding had been fast and furious. It seemed everyone in the whole world was intent on owning a piece of Clapton. (Indeed, it would later be reported that although the auction's organizers had initially hoped to raise approximately $750,000 total, the event actually tallied up $5,072,350.)

I began to worry. I was usually comfortable with having a maximum spending lid in place when I bid at auctions—after all, what responsible individual or arts institution doesn't do it that way? But sales figures averaging four times their estimates? At that rate we would likely acquire neither of the two targeted guitars. Bruce and I discussed. He was new at this big-time auction stuff and heard me out about my growing concerns. And so, after the second report came in from New York bearing the same sort of alarming message, we both knew something had to be done.

He ran over to his desk and began trying to call Jody and Paul to seek their input. No luck. Paul was out of town. Jody was boarding a plane somewhere. They were effectively incommunicado. And all I could think of was two things: I had never before superceded agreed-upon bidding limits, and I really didn't care to do that now. But complicating matters was the very last thing Paul had said to me regarding Brownie when we'd bumped into each other in the hallway a day or two prior: "So, Pete, you really think we can find good ways of using that guitar?" "Yes, I do" was my reply. "Well, then: let's *get* it."

The telling moment finally arrived: Lot 98 would be coming up in about two minutes. Fine. I'd be ready to bid all the way up to my limit, which was something above the estimated value. I could hear their auctioneer bellowing the usual auction patter, starting the bidding, and getting a flurry of bids. A flurry? No, more like a tidal wave. Seemingly within seconds the bidding had raced right on past the $20,000 to $30,000 estimate, rocketing to the unbelievable sum of $90,050—a figure well beyond my agreed-upon uppermost limit.

Meanwhile, I just stood there slack-jawed. I'd failed to even blurt out a single bid before other bidders left me in the dust. This was not looking good. I turned to Bruce and explained the dire circumstances. He ran back to his desk and made more attempts to get advice from his new bosses. No luck. That's when I mentioned Paul's instructions to me. Though I thought I had a fairly clear grasp of the English language, somehow I was suddenly getting a bit wobbly, and my brain was trying to resist the realization that "get it" in fact had a quite exact meaning. And so we came up with a plan. Since we didn't get Lot 98, perhaps we could reasonably apply the funds budgeted for it straight to the sum budgeted for Lot 105, Brownie, and at least still have some chance at snagging our priority guitar.

This would mean bending the normal rules—and in a rather dramatic way—but what else to do under these strange circumstances? Then came the moment of truth: I braced myself to try and be more aggressive in bidding. I listened in panicked silence as Lot 103 sold for an astounding $211,500. And then, Lot 104 for $101,500! This was getting ridiculous. The auction crowd was abuzz and then suddenly came the opening riffs of "Layla," and a huge roar and waves of applause erupted as they unveiled Brownie.

The auctioneer tried to calm the room down, and then, clear as a bell, he blurted out most giddily, "Well! I don't even know where to begin with this one!" In response, one smart aleck shouted out "$200," and the crowd roared with glee. A news account later reported that from there things got serious quickly, noting that "Initially, it went up in increments of $20,000." Well, perhaps so, but amid all the din the very first thing I heard was someone yelling out, "$80,000!" Then another bid $100,000.

Not to be bypassed so quickly this time, I weighed in with $200,000. Mind you, the auctioneer was not even in control at this point. We, the bidders, were ignoring all decorum—or even standard auction-house bidding increments. Then another bidder shouted, "$300,000!" In a sweaty, dazed state, I pushed the price all the way up to $400,000. And in making that leap I'd officially and completely surpassed any "reasonable" limits we'd ever discussed at EMP.

At that sobering point, the pace slowed a bit, pausing for a time at $420,000. Reportedly, the auctioneer jokingly offered to throw in a guitar stand as a bonus. The auction resumed and the crowd roared again when bidding stopped at $478,000. They understood that with the hammer's fall, history had been made, and the most expensive auction transaction ever for a guitar had concluded. Moments later, with my hands drenched in sweat, I plopped down on the corner of my desk and turned to Bruce: "We got it."

What a complex emotional state I was in: elation mixed with foreboding apprehension. In the end I had gone beyond not only our original planned budget, but even beyond our little emergency scheme to give it our best go by combining the budgets for both guitars into one last stab at nabbing Brownie. Indeed, I'd gone quite a bit further than even I'd thought was sensible. Our bosses needed to be apprised of the news: that my final winning bid had been "successful"—and with the Christie's buyer's premium tacked on, EMP was now on the hook for $497,500.

In the meantime, the auction had sparked a global media frenzy. Speculation was running rampant about who could have been the secret winning bidder. I cringed a little when I read somewhere that this "new sales record" had surpassed the old one previously held by "another Fender Stratocaster, the white model played by Jimi Hendrix during his appearance at Woodstock." The bloodhounds— whether they knew it yet or not—were already sniffing down the correct trail: straight to Paul Allen.

At day's end I went home feeling fairly calm considering all that excitement. And maybe Bruce did as well. But all I know is that the first thing the next morning, he came in and looked a bit under the weather. He confessed that he'd lain awake all night worrying that we would both be in trouble. I felt just awful and tried to assure him that if there was trouble, I alone could be faulted for having gone wild in the bidding. He was new here and had really just been a spectator. But such assurances probably didn't help much. The only thing that would resolve his concerns would be a response from our employers.

Luckily, that occurred before too many hours went by. When told of the "success" at this auction, we both received nothing but supportive words from both Paul and Jody. If they were the least bit upset, they shielded the two of us from any scorn. As the hours passed and word spread within EMP, the top ranks on down were thrilled and sent e-mail messages of congratulations. As usual, the whole team was committed to keeping the fact of our famous new acquisition an in-house secret—one that our PR team would announce only when the moment was right.

But major coverage of the event continued, with that spectacular auction finale being repeatedly broadcast by the likes of CNN, VH-1, and MTV's news programs. Within a couple days after the auction, VH-1 began spreading the rumor that Brownie had been bought by Paul Allen "for his planned rock 'n' roll museum in Seattle." How, exactly, the secret first leaked remains a mystery, but from there the gossip accelerated throughout the broadcast and print media.

And so, with all that free publicity swirling around the globe, EMP responded by cannily taking advantage of it, in part by sending me out to talk it up with select reporters—a brilliant tactic that ultimately helped cement an image in the public's expectant mind that when EMP did finally open its doors, the place would be chock-full of rock 'n' roll's finest treasures.

Sure enough, *Guitar World* magazine later published a feature article titled "House of the Holy—Bow Down, True Believer, and Enter the Hallowed Halls of the Experience Music Project . . . Home to Such Sacred Artifacts as . . . Eric Clapton's Layla Strat and the World's Largest Collection of Jimi Hendrix Memorabilia." The article noted that the Brownie sales figure "was significantly more than Blecha was authorized to pay, but the curator admits he got carried away as auction bidding soared. 'I got the fever,' he confesses."

▶ Rare promotional poster for a Jimi Hendrix Experience concert at the Seattle Center Coliseum on May 23, 1969.

PICTURES OF AN EXHIBITION

09

SEATTLE CENTER COLISEUM
FRIDAY, MAY 23 / 8:30 PM

JIMI HENDRIX
EXPERIENCE

A CONCERTS WEST PRESENTATION

TICKETS at FIDELITY LANE & SUBURBAN OUTLETS

5⁵⁰/4⁷⁵/3⁷⁵/2⁷⁵

THE HENDRIX GALLERY

By 1998 EMP's exhibit development efforts were fully under way. It was reassuring to realize that, although we would continue to collect interesting rock 'n' roll artifacts, the vast majority of items needed to fill out the numerous galleries were safely tucked away in our high-security vault. Still, just as it's the missing items in any series that drive the completist collector nuts, those as-yet-unfound items were creating the most pressure on me as deadlines approached.

For example, while it seemed a given that the central displays in the Hendrix Gallery would be anchored by some of the crown jewels of the collection—the Woodstock Stratocaster; the wah-wah, Octavia, and Univibe pedals; and an amplifier that I had acquired from a longtime Hendrix collector in England—it didn't seem right or accurate to present all this without a serious nod to the guitarist's bandmates as well. After all, the Jimi Hendrix Experience had been a trio, not a solo venture.

This desire to be fair and to not fixate on Hendrix at the expense of his creative collaborators constituted a serious problem. Noel Redding had long ago sold off his original, much-used Fender Jazz bass and amp and other relevant materials to fanatical Hendrix disciples/collectors. The possibility of ever turning up that stuff in time was thin. And then there was the matter of Mitch Mitchell and his various drum sets. For many years, all reports indicated that Jimi's former drummer was now a sort of international man of mystery. He'd rarely popped up anywhere, and was often rumored to be in France, or Morocco, or God knows where. Unlike with Redding, I hadn't had any contact with Mitchell whatsoever and had no idea how to make that contact. In simple truth—and though it may sound cold—what I needed was not direct communications with him. What I needed was his stuff.

▶ A circa-1968 King Vox-Wah (model #95-932011) distortion pedal formerly owned by Jimi Hendrix.

With hope and faith, we moved forward at EMP with the design of a stagelike setting for the Woodstock Strat and all—and I kept my ear to the rail for any slight rumors of where Redding's and Mitchell's instruments were hiding out. Then we got a lucky break. I received a call from a well-known Hendrix collector with whom I'd been in contact for years—in fact, way back in the 1970s he'd actually lived in Seattle before moving back East. His message was one delivered to grateful ears: creeping age and changing priorities had convinced him that it was time to liquidate his massive Hendrix collection. Best of all was the surprise news that it had been he who'd bought Redding's gear so many years ago. EMP would get first shot at it before the items were put up for public auction. A deal was struck, both parties made happy, and now the exhibit had only that one other hole: no physical objects that represented Mitchell's contributions.

With two-thirds of the puzzle complete, this missing portion caused a curatorial ache that grew as the months passed and the finality of those dreaded deadlines approached. But there was nothing to do about it. All leads went dry. All tips dead-ended. My myriad efforts to reach Mitchell failed. Tick-tock went the clock, and I resigned myself to the idea that we'd done our best and the exhibit would still be great. As it was, the Hendrix Gallery boasted hundreds of other pieces of eye candy: Hendrix's own tour diary, handwritten lyrics, iconic stage

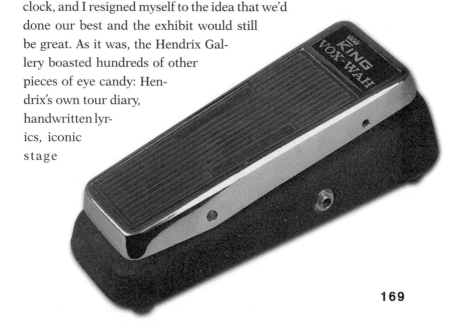

apparel (like the famous turquoise kimono), rare psychedelic concert posters, photographs, performance film footage, oral history testimonials, gold records, and on and on . . .

I was just about ready to give up hope when the impossible happened again. My trusty telephone rang, and on the other end was a British bloke who wanted to sell Mitch Mitchell's black Ludwig drums—the very kit he had played at Woodstock—a peculiar and custom-selected assortment of drums configured with rather unusual hardware. This was fabulous news, if in fact the claims were true. So the grilling began, and, long story short, the trail of ownership proved to be legit. The seller had acquired the drums after they'd been donated by Mitchell to a British charity auction numerous years before. Now this winning bidder at that auction was offering them up, and EMP suddenly found itself the proud owner of the last and final piece of the power-trio puzzle.

Beyond the high quality of individual artifacts, the worth of the final Hendrix exhibit would of course rely on the conceptual constructs that would frame it. In determining the themes for the gallery, we definitely faced some challenges. Because of the plethora of biographies and documentaries about Jimi's life, the central challenge was how to shape an exhibit story line into something that added value to yet one more exploration of the topic. The solution that emerged was to offer minimal biographical information (and devote no attention whatsoever to his demise). We would instead focus on highlights of his career as an active musician, and track and interpret his numerous creative contributions to the world of music.

It took a ton of effort by a lot of people, but by late spring 2000—the gallery prepared, the artifacts mounted, our oral history interviews edited into films, and the multimedia content powered up—our team figured that we'd done Jimi proud. The entire gallery was a visually beautiful place that went way beyond straight biography and actually explored meaningful topics, like the chain of musical influences that had affected Hendrix, his formidable songwriting skills, and his role as a pioneer in the usage of electronic distortion devices (their use in his music actually made history by retraining the public's ears to accept and enjoy cutting-edge, if challenging, sounds). In short, I believe the Hendrix Gallery perfectly embodied EMP's mission to "celebrate creativity and innovation" in music.

QUEST FOR VOLUME

Quest for Volume is what I eventually named EMP's exhibit dedicated to the history of the guitar. The gallery ultimately took the form of a chronological display of fifty-five instruments that effectively related major outlines of the story of the emergence (and eventual popularity) of that newfangled musical tool, the electric guitar.

The exhibit name derived from what I figured to be the core dynamic in this history: that since the guitar's initial emergence in Europe a few centuries ago, its main problem had been that it was a relatively small, and thus quiet, instrument. As a result, the crucial design imperative since day one has been for luthiers to discover ways to build louder instruments.

By tracing that design history—and the impact various innovations would subsequently have on the sound of music—our visitors could see more than three hundred years of guitar evolution unfold: from ancient and tiny, heavily inlaid cat-gut strung Italian guitar up through a final section called "The Cutting Edge," which highlighted recent state-of-the-art instrument design and featured way-out units like a Wright SoloEtte guitar (the preferred instrument of NASA astronauts, who have hauled one along into outer space).

In between these two temporal bookends were displayed prime examples of just about every important guitar model built in the intervening years. Some of them are true gems, like an impossibly

rare 1834 guitar handmade by C. F. Martin, and
also the oldest known guitar made by Orville Gibson himself. This 1897 Gibson instrument helps
us see the historic moment when steel strings first
replaced cat gut, a technological advance that
on its own required bigger guitars with stronger
internal bracing designs. Then there were amazing
examples of other pre–Electric Age efforts
to increase the instrument's volume via
mechanical solutions—for example, the
ultrarare guitar made in the early twentieth
century by Augustus Stroh, who sought to solve
the volume issue by attaching a large and shiny
metal megaphone-like horn to his instrument.

One of my personal favorite displays was an
assortment of the earliest electric guitars (and
amplifiers) to ever be marketed. These were all lap
steels, a peculiar class of instrument so named for
two good reasons: first, they are meant to be
played flat on one's lap (as opposed to the standard, more common, Spanish strumming style),
and second, one hand picks in the usual fashion,
but the other holds a small metal bar that slides
up and down the strings to make that trademark
keening sound associated with Hawaiian music
and later with country-western music. The
gem of EMP's lap steels was a one- of-a-kind
Gibson. Not just an example of their first
marketed model, this historic specimen
is the actual "test mule" that Gibson's staff
designers and electrical engineers used on
the company's workbench during early efforts
in 1935 to perfect an electrical pickup. In effect,

this guitar is physical evidence of industrial design creativity, of pure innovation and invention.

Though every guitar (and matching amplifier) in the gallery has admirable qualities—and each represents its own acquisition adventure—a few others remain real favorites. Among those is the 1933 Dobro All-Electric, a guitar credited as probably the first electrified Spanish-style (as opposed to the Hawaiian-style lap steels) ever marketed. Rumors say that only two or three of these have survived. That I reeled this one in by perusing the classified ads in *Vintage Guitar* magazine, I think, fully justifies the many hundreds of hours that were devoted to this not-unpleasant aspect of the guitar-collecting "task."

Another individual instrument with an amazing tale of discovery is one of the K&F brand lap steels that dates to the mid-1940s—and whose key importance is its relationship to the revered Fender legacy. As is widely known, the Fender company was founded in the late 1940s by a Fullerton, California, radio repair shop owner named Leo Fender. Prior to that, Fender and a partner—a vaudeville-era steel guitar veteran named "Doc" Kauffman—had made and sold a number of electric lap steels under the brand name K&F.

I'd known that EMP needed to acquire one of these K&F guitars, and so I'd been shopping around for a few years looking for just the right museum-quality specimen. One day, someone sent me a photograph of a K&F that was quite different from the others I'd seen. In fact, it was downright odd looking, with an unusual body shape, a unique paint finish, and a volume knob and pickup assembly that were different. At the same time, it didn't appear to be altered or modified. The thing seemed old as the hills. As I like nothing better than a good history mystery, my curiosity was piqued.

Then I remembered a photograph published in Richard R. Smith's *Fender: The Sound Heard 'Round the World*. Racing to EMP's library shelf, I paged through it and, sure enough, right there was an

---

◀ Ultrarare circa-1920 Stroh recording guitar with metal ampliphonic horn hand-engraved by the maker, Augustus Stroh of England.

image of an identical lap steel, which Smith had described as one of the very earliest K&F models ever made. I wasted no time, struck the deal, and anxiously awaited its arrival at EMP's offices.

Before the guitar showed up, I got on the horn with Smith. He'd interviewed both Fender and Kauffman years before, and they'd related that K&F had started out in 1945 during World War II. The two partners' initial efforts were crimped because of wartime rationing of critical materials like certain metals, wire, and even magnets. Out of necessity the duo had been forced to scrounge materials in order to construct their guitars. So it was that the electromagnetic pickups they'd installed in their first four or five lap steels were built with recycled magnets yanked from old Ford Model T engines at a nearby wrecking yard.

This was all interesting information in a trivia sort of way. But, in fact, it all added up after the K&F guitar arrived. Inspecting the thing, I noticed that nestled amid all the guts was a most remarkable thing: a guitar pickup whose magnet bore an unforgettable iconic corporate logo, a four-letter word as clear as day: Ford. Today, visitors to EMP can behold one of the oldest surviving instruments handmade by Leo Fender himself.

There were, of course, other notable instruments to be displayed—a one-of-a-kind 1957 design-phase prototype of the famous 1958 Gibson Flying V certainly comes to mind—but then again, I loved *all* these babies. The one other instrument that I really must share a story about, however, is actually an electric bass guitar—the Audiovox 736 Bass Fiddle.

As a subset of the Quest for Volume exhibit, I developed a display about how the electric bass was created and how its invention had a dramatic effect on music. The instrument has been credited with allowing R&B, rock 'n' roll, funk, and reggae to come into being. The display set the stage with a precursor to the electric bass, a circa-1850 European upright acoustic double bass.

From there the display traced the few visionary companies that tried to electrify upright basses with rare and exceedingly freaky experimental units, such as the minimalist sticklike 1936 Vega Electric Bass and an ultrarare (two of a kind) 1937 Gibson. Design evolution was, of course, heading toward a historically radical iteration of these electrified basses—a quantum advance resulting in an ergonomically sized instrument that was played horizontally instead of upright, literally transforming the bass into a bass *guitar*. The instrument that had long been given credit for being the world's first electric bass guitar was the beautiful, crackly, butterscotch-finished 1952 Fender Precision. But my research into guitar history upset this conventional wisdom.

Displayed chronologically between the Vega and the Gibson was another instrument. It was electric. A bass. A guitar. And I have been credited with making its discovery, a discovery that made obsolete all previously published histories of the electric bass guitar.

Here's how it all happened: My interest in Audiovox instruments dates back to my 1970s Budget Records days when I befriended a customer named Jim Basnight, who led a U District band called the Moberlys. While chatting in the shop one day, he mentioned that a fellow student up at Roosevelt High School by the name of Tutmarc had always made the preposterous claim that his grandfather had invented the electric guitar right here in Seattle way back in the 1930s. Sure, right.

How could that be true? If it was, then you'd think we'd all know about it, MOHAI would have mounted some exhibit about it, or the Chamber of Commerce would have promoted the heck out of the "fact." A few years later, when I mounted a 50 Years of Hit-Making in the Pacific Northwest exhibit at Peaches Records, an older gentleman showed up, introduced himself as Bud Tutmarc, handed me a stack of family photos, and said that long ago his father, Paul, had invented the electric guitar and had marketed them out of Seattle under the Audiovox brand name. In fact, Bud went on, to this day he was an active musician touring the world playing Hawaiian steel-guitar music on one of his deceased father's old guitars.

Intrigued but still rather skeptical, I listened and looked. Sure enough, the aged photos seemed to show the Tutmarc family band in the 1930s with Paul playing an electric lap steel, his wife Lorraine playing some kind of weird electric four-string instrument, and a much-younger Bud strumming an acoustic guitar. Informed that Paul Tutmarc had begun tinkering with electrifying various household instruments back in 1930–31—the time period, I knew, that Adolph "The Inventor of the Electric Guitar" Rickenbacker had been doing the same thing in Los Angeles—the inner detective in me was now on full alert.

Over the following years I conducted much research in an attempt to verify or debunk Bud's claims. Along the way I dug up more than thirty Audiovox guitars and amplifiers at junk shops, at garage sales, and even at a number of guitar shops that placed little value on these oddball mystery instruments. Hell, nobody but me seemed to want them, so dealers happily cut me deals, first in the $50 range, then $75, and on up. The most recent one I spied was on eBay—it sold for $1,800. But what refused to pop up was one of those four-stringers as seen in that old family photo.

Then one day my phone rang at EMP. On the other end was a fellow who'd long been a helpful source for locating interesting guitars of all types. He knew I had a fetish for these Audiovox oddities, so he was a bit excited when he told me that he'd just grabbed one at a flea market and was hoping I'd be interested. "I just picked this up from some little old lady who thought it was a lap steel. And it may be. But it's a weird one, with a longer neck than usual, and only four strings."

Forty-five minutes later I was at his place, took a quick look, struck a deal, and added the only Audiovox bass guitar then known to exist straight into EMP's collection. I also now felt safe about spreading the word to, and seeking opinions from, a number of the world's top guitar historians. When I shared my research about Paul

Tutmarc and his Audiovox company, they agreed that the only reasonable conclusion was that my work had just overthrown decades
of accepted history. Seattle's Paul Tutmarc had been an early pioneer
of electric guitars, and his circa-1936 Electric Bass Fiddle deserved
recognition as an important milestone in guitar design history.

Asked to write up its history, I composed a detailed account—
"Discovered! The World's First Electric Bass Guitar"—that became

▲ A rare matching set of circa-1935, Seattle-made Audiovox electric steel guitar and amplifier.

the cover feature for *Vintage Guitar* magazine in March 1999. Also included was a companion essay, penned by guitar historian John Teagle, titled "The Fender Myth Debunked." Because the ever-skeptical Teagle had devoted years to conducting "extensive research into the early days of electric and electrified musical instruments," he had initially not been "wholly convinced" about my conclusions. Given that "in this day and age, any great revelation regarding the history of American guitars is met with suspicion," he went on to say that "perhaps this essay should have been titled 'Audiovox vs. the Piltdown Man,' due to the doubts had by myself and a number of others regarding the authenticity of" my claims. I found this effort to contextualize the significance of my discoveries by invoking an historic archaeological reference —that of the elaborate 1912 "discovery" of the "missing link" remains of an extinct hominid in Piltdown, England—to be particularly pleasing.

Especially as Teagle was contrasting the two cases. "The Piltdown Man, for those who played guitar all day instead of doing your anthropology homework, represents the ultimate hoax on a scientific community—a deliberate deceit." My Audiovox research, on the other hand, now demands that "any accolades previously bestowed upon Mr. Fender for inventing the [electric] bass must instead be placed posthumously upon Paul Tutmarc." History, it seems, had been officially rewritten.

So, for history buffs who came to EMP, I made sure that there would be some good surprises. And for guitar freaks, there would be plenty of eye candy. But we also had the interests of music lovers in mind as Quest for Volume was organized. Like the museum's other exhibits, Quest would benefit greatly from its technological attributes—especially the gallery's audio and film content. The audio was to be delivered through headphone devices called Museum Exhibit Guides (MEGs), which would blend—via the creative skills of a new and very talented Multimedia Department team member named Bryan Yates—music, a master narrative, and snippets from our oral histories.

I believed that the narration—which was geared to mesh with my text labels—needed to be an authoritative voice, meaning a recognized guitar historian. In addition, we wanted that person to possess a naturally warm and inviting vocal tone. Luckily, I knew just who fit the bill: my buddy, Nashville-based Gibson-company historian, author, and musician Walter Carter. Carter accepted and did a splendid job of reviewing the labels and penning his own script, which augmented those themes with additional historical insights.

Added to this narration, our years of oral history efforts were about to really pay off, as Yates was able to extract quotes we'd captured from such luminaries as Les Paul, Chet Atkins, and C. F. Martin IV. Yates also oversaw recording sessions with a fabulous array of players who performed period-appropriate licks on our instruments. Musicians included old-timey experts Artie Traum and Bob Brozman, Hawaiian steeler Bud Tutmarc, jazz master Larry Coryell, eclecticist Bill Frisell, roots dude Taj Mahal, lap steeler Greg Leise, country chicken-picker Brent Mason, queen of the electric bass Carol Kaye, Living Colour's Vernon Reid, and others. This huge effort ensured that visitors would be able to actually hear music from every single instrument on display.

The other exhibit component that helped bring the whole thing to life was a wonderful movie produced by EMP's filmmaker, Kay

◀ The ultrarare circa-1936, Seattle-made Audiovox #736 model Electric Bass Fiddle.

Ray. We knew that the exhibit was still missing moving images of guitarists performing. My curatorial caveat was that any such images needed to be rare clips that people hadn't already seen a million times before. That was a big challenge, but Ray conducted an epic search and managed to track down much material that hadn't seen the light of day in many years, including vintage footage of ace guitarists like Son House, Andres Segovia, Les Paul and Mary Ford, Jimmy Bryant and Speedy West, Eddie Cochran, Albert King, Roy Buchanan, the Jeff Beck Group, Bonnie Raitt, and Derek and the Dominos.

In the end, after working for years toward the completion of this Quest for Volume exhibit, the team accomplished the creation of the world's first-ever comprehensive exhibit about the history of the electric guitar. As I told a reporter at Guitar.com, we hoped the exhibit would be meaningful to the public because it "tracks the technological innovations along the way in the rise of the electric guitar. There will be interesting things for guitar enthusiasts, but at the same time, for the neophytes, beyond seeing the chronological display of the changing materials and the physical design of the instruments, they'll also be exposed to the rise of electric music."

▲ The History of the Bass Guitar display in the Quest for Volume exhibit at EMP.

THE NORTHWEST PASSAGE

Much of the earliest European exploration of the New World was defined by a quest to discover a major waterway across North America that was for centuries imagined as the "Northwest Passage." At EMP, the Northwest Passage was the name I gave to the museum building's largest gallery space. As a major exhibit devoted to the story of the region's musical history, the Northwest Passage would in a very real way help define the institution's image in visitors' minds.

The organizing concept I developed for the Northwest Passage displays amounted to a linear exhibit that presented an overview of the high points of local music making. To bring some coherent order to a story line that would necessarily encompass a broad time span as well as a wide range of musical genres, the individual displays would be paced roughly chronologically. Like the Hendrix and guitar galleries, this one would also benefit greatly from multimedia content, including a series of video loops shown on monitors and MEG content that offered music along with a master narrative to help guide people through all the history.

From day one, I resisted suggestions by other staffers that I record this narration. In my view the Northwest Passage was special, perhaps more so than any of our other galleries. Unlike the Hendrix or guitar galleries, it would contain exhibits that strictly reflected the stories of our community. It would focus on the musical accomplishments of many still-living musicians, players whose bands in some cases were still active and individuals who knew their own stories far better than anyone else possibly could. This saga seemed best told in the words of these people themselves. Indeed, if ever there was an exhibit that shouldn't be saddled with museum-staple interpretation provided by that all-knowing pontificator otherwise known as a "curator," the Northwest Passage was it.

That decision proved to be a winner. It allowed us to solicit the help of many members of the music community, people who had been participants in or observers of this history as it was being made. We simply informed them about the themes being highlighted—the creativity and innovation that each era's musicians had contributed to the ongoing evolution of popular music—and cut them loose to record their own commentary about these events.

For example, when visitors entered the Northwest Passage gallery and encountered the "Humble Beginnings" display, they would see cool artifacts such as an old 1920s radio microphone and the actual 1940s equipment from one of Seattle's pioneering recording studios—

A portion of the Grunge Rock display in the Northwest Passage Gallery at EMP.

and they would hear MEG narration by Seattle's legendary king of 1960s radio, Pat O'Day, about the early days when our local "music industry" facilities were extremely primitive. An early fan of radio, O'Day was already working in the radio biz by 1959, when the very first local teenage group—Olympia High School's Fleetwoods—scored a number one national hit with their gentle doo-wop ballad "Come Softly to Me." Being a local record, cut in a local studio, and issued by a local label, the thing had blown the longstanding conventional wisdom that a hit record could never break out of the Northwest. When it actually happened, this out-of-the-blue success blew everybody's minds and really kick-started the area's music scene—suddenly everybody and their brother formed bands, opened studios, launched labels, and tried to duplicate that phenomenon. This remarkable pop-history moment is represented in a display that includes Kay Ray's fine video, which mixes the group performing live on Dick Clark's *American Bandstand* with various oral history clips, and cool artifacts such as old photographs, radio charts, the Fleetwoods' original gold record, and the actual dress worn by one of the singers on the album cover.

In a similar way, an adjacent display about Seattle's infamous and wild Jackson Street jazz scene (of the 1920s–50s) featured awesome artifacts I rounded up, such as Quincy Jones's 1940s trumpet from his youthful Seattle days; a copy of the first 78 record cut in 1948 by Seattle jazz diva Ernestine Anderson; and a rare photograph of the teenaged Ray Charles's early trio along with a copy of their debut 78 cut in Seattle in 1949. These physical items were augmented by another video (a blend of vintage performance and EMP oral history footage) and MEG narration by one of Seattle's beloved African-American jazz veterans, trumpeter Floyd Standifer.

Next to that was a display dedicated to the almost universally unknown story of our region's vintage R&B scene. Amazingly, a lot of people had no idea that back in the 1950s Seattle and Tacoma had many R&B bands and singers; my hope was to help change that fact. Exhibited here were rare records, photographs, and posters

183

representing doo-wop groups such as the Barons and the Gallahads, combos like Joe Boot and the Fabulous Winds (who honked out rockin' R&B like "That's Tough" in area nightclubs and on record), and even pioneering African-American DJs who spun R&B records on the air in the 1940s and '50s, such as Bob Summerise, who provided excellent MEG narration.

From here, the exhibit continued down a winding passagelike gallery space, where displays highlighted different phases in the evolutionary development of the region's rock traditions, an area that came to be widely known as the Northwest Sound. The artifacts included old dance posters, records, photos, and a locally made Thomas brand bass guitar used by the Wailers, the Tacoma-based band whose "Tall Cool One" had become a national hit right on the heels of the Fleetwoods' success back in 1959. In addition, there were lots of artifacts representing another Tacoma band, the Ventures, whose classic, "Walk—Don't Run," became an international phenomenon in 1960 and led to their eventual recognition as the world's top instrumental rock 'n' roll band. Northwest Passage represents their story with very cool stuff such as guitarist Nokie Edwards's stage jacket, copies of their rarest early records, radio charts, band photos, and an example of the scarce Mosrite brand of a mid-1960s Ventures-model electric guitar.

Then came one of the centerpieces of the whole gallery. It represented two bands and one of the prime tales of Northwest rock history, the saga of "Louie Louie." One display conveyed how several local 1960s teen R&B bands recorded that old 1950s R&B chestnut and turned it into the region's signature song. But the display goes further. It also includes the ensuing drama of how Paul Revere and the Raiders and the Kingsmen dueled with competing versions during the summer of 1963 on competing Portland, Oregon, radio stations—and then, after an internal tiff, the Kingsmen actually broke up. But in late 1963 the Kingsmen's record became a left-field smash hit on Boston radio and broke out on the *Billboard* charts.

This surprise success caused the band to re-form (with a few new members) in order to milk their good fortune.

In early 1964, rumors surfaced in the media that the record contained "filthy," or even "pornographic," lyrics. The governor of Indiana urged a ban on further radio airplay in his state, sparking a media frenzy. With parents complaining, the FBI, the U.S. Postal Service, and even the Federal Trade Commission all launched formal investigations into the song. It's a ridiculous and quite entertaining tale—much too long to relate here. The critical fact is that, after two years of digging, the FBI's investigation ended with the conclusion that the Kingsmen's little 45 could not be considered pornographic because—its staff having dutifully tried to play it every which way (faster at 78 rpm, and slower at 33⅓ rpm)—the darn thing was simply, and I quote from the FBI's own files, "unintelligible at any speed."

The saga of "Louie Louie" is a recognized classic from Northwest rock history, and it therefore needed a special display setting. So I asked the Van Sickle and Rolleri design team, which was working for us, to come up with a setting to be called "The Battle of the Bands." To my great pleasure, they perfectly captured the look of a typical *American Graffiti*–era 1960s high-school gym stage that could showcase various stage apparel and instruments used by the two battling bands.

Filling that stage with quality artifacts proved to be a tough challenge. Having already acquired my former collection of materials, EMP was well stocked on the record, poster, radio chart, and band photograph fronts, but we still needed significant items— preferably original musical instruments and the like. One major breakthrough occurred serendipitously. A fellow in Portland had bought from the original owner the entire recording studio where both the Raiders and the Kingsmen had cut their respective "Louie Louie" 45s thirtysome years before. He offered up for sale the original Neumann 4-47 microphone used in those sessions. After I verified the seller's story with the original owner/engineer, Bob Lindahl, I struck the deal.

"Louie Louie"—Play It Again, and Again

Local Northwest bands virtually performed the crowds' favorites at teen dances, and one obscure "Louie Louie" R&B tune captured the white kids' fancy more than any other. "Louie Louie," its hypnotic beat and catchy lyrics about a love-lorn sailor made it the one song required of every band, every night, at every dance.

The Northwest's trademark song, rock 'n' roll that wouldn't die

Despite heavy-handed FBI and FCC investigations, a mid-sixties radio ban and multiple lawsuits, the garage-rock anthem "Louie Louie" has been recorded by more than 1000 bands.

THE BEST OF
LOUIE, LOUIE

DANCE
Jamboree & Stage Show
Salem Armory
FRIDAY EVE. • APRIL 21
The Wailers
Rockin' Robin Roberts
and
Gail Harris
$1.25

"Louie Louie"

A simple song. A serious scandal.
"Dirty" lyrics? Or imaginations run amok?

Another item I figured would be interesting would be a copy of the FBI's old investigative file. Other researchers had pried it loose earlier by invoking the Freedom of Information Act, and I followed suit. But the Feds apparently weren't all that happy about my plans. My effort to acquire the thing took, as I recall, about four different letters of request mailed over a two-year time span.

The file did eventually arrive, but my plan to display it alongside an original 1964 set of officially published "Louie Louie" sheet music—so that museum visitors could compare the many versions of the song's alleged nasty words (that the FBI had collected from paranoid parents) with the actual lyrics—proved problematic. The documents in the 126-page FBI file contained such utterly vile renditions of the lyrics, there was no way we could conceive of displaying them in a family-friendly museum. Instead, we ended up selecting a few of the interesting (though mostly profanity-free) pages and mounted them next to the sheet music with the perfectly clean lyrics as actually sung by the Kingsmen.

Though these pieces were fun and kind of cool, these items were still not adding up to the exhibit I'd hoped for. We needed to find things like instruments, gold records, concert tour programs—significant material like that, and lots of it! Being acquainted with a few of the Kingsmen, my search naturally began with them. Unfortunately, their initial responses were not encouraging. As I was to learn, not much remained from the old days. But then my friend (and their keyboardist/guitarist) Barry Curtis confessed that he did still have one old 1960s stage jacket tucked away that we could borrow. While this Kingsmen puzzle remained a bit frustrating, I shifted gears and started at the other end: by working on the Raiders.

One of the first members I reached was Phil "Fang" Volk. Luckily, and after much persuasion, he proved willing to sell EMP his original old white Vox Phantom IV bass guitar (the one he flipped over

◄ The Northwest Passage display at EMP, featuring the original Fender Stratocaster used on the Kingsmen's 1963 hit, "Louie Louie."

each week on ABC TV's *Where the Action Is* to show the audience his nickname, Fang, plastered on the backside in big black letters). To sweeten our deal, he even threw in one of his old stage costumes.

Then I made arrangements to fly down to Reno, Nevada, to meet up with the band's namesake keyboardist/leader, Paul Revere, who took me on a tour of his shuttered oldies-themed nightclub and generously allowed me to select items for loan—his old bright-red Vox organ, one of his signature tricornered colonial-style hats, a gold record, and an early dance poster.

Still shy of good Kingsmen items, I began hitting on other members and ex-members, eventually working my way to drummer Dick Peterson. Though perfectly friendly, he unfortunately said about the same thing I had already been hearing: "There's really not that much left anymore." But, he added, if we were interested, he still had his original drum set replete with the band's logo painted on the bass drum head. Well, once we got into this discussion, and he really wracked his brain, Peterson came up with a few more goodies such as a gold record for the "Louie Louie" single and one for the *Louie Louie* LP—oh, and the original Fender Stratocaster guitar that his bandmate, Mike Mitchell, had actually used back in 1963 while recording the famous song.

The tides were finally turning in my search. But wait a minute: how in the hell did he—the Kingsmen's drummer—happen to have Mitchell's "Louie Louie" guitar?" It seemed too good to be true. As Peterson explained, way back at the end of 1963, Mitchell traded in the Strat at a Portland music shop in order to get a new guitar. At the same time Peterson was playing drums in a different band, and also wanted to learn guitar. It just so happened that his parents took him to that same shop, and while selling the Strat to the Petersons, the salesman mentioned whose guitar it had been. Funny thing is, just a few weeks later Peterson was asked to join the Kingsmen. He stowed the guitar away and subsequently worked as their drummer for decades. As Peterson related all this to me, I was floored. Few early guitar solos from the classic era of garage rock stack up to the chaotic one Mitchell played on "Louie Louie" with this very guitar. You want a rock 'n' roll icon? Here it was! I believed that no matter what, EMP needed to exhibit this instrument. First things first, though: I got Mitchell's verification that it was the correct guitar. Then Peterson and I met up, he let me test-drive a few "Louie Louie" chords on it, and we cut a package deal for the guitar and his gold records. The display was shaping up quite nicely when the dam broke loose and even more goodies started shakin' out of the woodwork: Barry Curtis's 1966 Hammond M-3 organ turned up from a third party, and even my pal in Nashville, George Gruhn, came up with a former Kingsmen's Gibson EB-3 bass guitar to add to the mix.

Critical mass was achieved, the accumulation of artifacts was amazing, and the whole display would be topped off with a very hip video produced by a talented filmmaker named Darek Mazzone. Titled *Battle of the Bands*, this piece includes vintage footage of both the Kingsmen and the Raiders performing "Louie Louie," intercut with EMP oral history interviews. The film is also spiced up with plenty of trashy black-and-white 1950s images of teenage house-party dances and J. Edgar Hoover and FBI agents knocking on doors and flashing badges.

After "The Battle of the Bands," the next displays were also artifact-rich and represented later high points in Northwest music history: the concurrent rise of the heavy metal and punk scenes in the 1970s and '80s. The former was represented by a lot of flamboyant and colorful stage apparel and guitars loaned to EMP by Ann and Nancy Wilson of Seattle's metal pioneers, Heart. Clustered with these artifacts were numerous other outfits, guitars, and even a huge set of drums from Queensrÿche, along with more from other popular headbangers like Rail and Metal Church. Overhead rolled a fantastic film (again by Mazzone) composed of vintage footage of these bands performing, along with oral history interviews; the display was capped by spirited MEG narration from Seattle's reigning metal expert/journalist, Jeff Gilbert. The exhibit design goal for this section was to evoke the pomposity of heavy metal, and when a reporter for the *Boston Globe* later criticized the whole setup as "a stupefying altar to the memory of Heart," I knew our team had accomplished our mission. Posed in snotty defiance of this mainstream metal tableaux was the gritty punk-rock display. In an obvious stylistic countertrend to metal, the story of Seattle and Portland's early punk-rock subculture featured a group of raggedy contrarians who rejected the metal scene's flash-pot, smoke-machine, and showbiz excesses in favor of a politicized back-to-basics approach. As such, the punk pioneers found it difficult to get any breaks from local club owners, local radio, or the local print media. It was a do-it-yourself uprising both by choice and by necessity—and one represented in the gallery with rare posters, self-issued records, photos, and several guitars from trailblazing bands like the Cheaters, the Wipers, and the Enemy. Best of all was the narration, recorded by a then-young witness to the scene, Mudhoney's Mark Arm.

The artifacts used in the hip-hop history display were just as interesting. Once again, because EMP had acquired my former collection, the items available for inclusion were vast. But to represent the rise of the Northwest's hip-hop scene—especially the emergence of the region's biggest hit-making rapper, Sir Mix-A-Lot—we asked for Sir Mix-A-Lot's help. He came through with a loan of his trademark *Mack Daddy* coat and Stetson hat. Surrounding those items would be things like turntables, a microphone, posters, photos, and lots of records and CDs from numerous popular artists, all telling the story of the phenomenal success of Seattle's Nastymix label and the subsequent explosion of other local hip-hop labels. Adding the perfect vibe to the display would be another Mazzone film that blended great music with oral history commentary by various luminaries of the scene, as well as MEG narration contributed by local tastemaker MC Wordsayer.

The final series of displays not only comprised the largest subsection of the Northwest Passage, but also boasted what was probably the best selection of historic artifacts. These displays documented the rise of the grunge-rock movement and, because they had been in planning for almost as long as the Hendrix gallery, the end result benefited from all that developmental lead time. For six years I'd been collecting grunge artifacts specifically for EMP. Added to that was my former collection, which contained hundreds of early grunge items dating back to the movement's first ripples around 1985. The combined pool of artifacts to choose from was the finest archive of such materials in existence.

The grunge displays were thus able to show some of the earliest posters documenting the earliest gigs by the earliest bands that can be considered part of the grunge school. For example, there were posters for bands like Green River (who begat Mudhoney), and Malfunkshun (who begat Mother Love Bone, who begat Pearl Jam). Amid the Malfunkshun and Mudhoney guitars, we mounted the original studio recording console (and tape deck and speaker monitors) that engineering whiz Jack Endino had used to cut all those pioneering Sub Pop grunge sessions with the aforementioned bands and newcomers like Nirvana, the Screaming Trees, and Soundgarden. In terms of Soundgarden materials, after years of delay—and at nearly the last second before the final deadlines struck—the band finally came through with a loan of some handwritten lyrics by singer Chris Cornell, and Kim Thayil kindly loaned us his white Guild S-100 Deluxe.

Filling out the rest of these numerous large display cases were tons of other cool grunge-era items: handwritten lyrics by Kurt Cobain; a cluster of Nirvana's guitars, bass, and drums; a Fender Stratocaster that Pearl Jam's Mike McCready smashed in concert in 1995; a guitar and bass from the Screaming Trees; a guitar from Green River/Mother Love Bone; Soundgarden and Alice in Chains gold records, posters, and photos; and much more. All this was supported by two different films by Mazzone, featuring performance

191

footage and oral history interviews with Krist Novoselic, Sub Pop's Bruce Pavitt, and other grunge insiders. Informed and witty MEG narration was provided by both Endino and Dawn Anderson, the founder/editor of an early grunge-era magazine, *Backlash*.

Lastly—and because by EMP's 2000 opening, grunge was already seen as a phenomenon that had long since peaked—I decided we needed to have a display called "Northwest Now." Here was our chance to acknowledge that a number of nongrunge bands had also found considerable success in recent years, and that a whole *new* stream of great bands were just starting to break out. So, among guitars, stage apparel, posters, photos, and one last film, we presented some music and information about popular bands like the Young Fresh Fellows, the Posies, Sleater-Kinney, and the Presidents of the United States of America, who were represented with a smashed and mangled candy apple–red Flying V guitar and some silly gold spray-painted boots.

My overarching hope for the Northwest Passage exhibit was that visitors would gain a stronger sense of the Northwest music scene's evolution down through the decades—and that this would be accomplished by considering the contributions made by both musicians and the many other professionals who form its artistic community. As I once told a *News Tribune* reporter, the goal was "to get away from star-worship. The history of Northwest music is not just about the stars, it's also about the record producers, the designers who created the posters, and the people who had the moxie to start a record label in the Northwest when everyone else said 'Forget it.'" Mostly though, I wanted visitors to EMP's Northwest Passage to experience a series of exhibits that were, well, unforgettable.

▶ The grungy Superfuzz stompbox, as battle-tested by Mark Arm of Mudhoney.

MILESTONES

THE GRAND OPENING

With my years of work on the museum's exhibits finally completed, I took on a few other final tasks for EMP's grand opening in June 2000. The least significant of these—but in some silly way perhaps the most fun—was "curating" a soundtrack for the Seattle Center's International Fountain. In the four decades since it first began spouting and spraying during Seattle's 1962 World's Fair, the fountain had, I was told, never been programmed in synchronization with a rock 'n' roll music soundtrack. I was invited to create one, and I most certainly jumped at the opportunity.

Having suffered through shows at the fountain that featured recorded classical music or Broadway show tunes, I have to admit that it felt downright subversive to get this crack at rockin' the place a little. I began outlining two possibilities, both of which drew exclusively on the music of local artists (Hendrix included). Option one was to sequence a selection of full-length songs that might be cool for people to listen to. Option two was to graft together a seamless aural collage of a longer list of song snippets. The merits of the first choice boiled down to artistic integrity, or rather, not inflicting editing violence on whole pieces of musical art. The second offered a chance to cut to the chase by linking the best, most dramatic portions of songs by a greater number of artists.

With the help of my pal, EMP's highly skilled audio engineer John Seman, we mocked up the two variations for analysis. In the end, the collage was approved by the Center's director, Virginia Anderson. It included excerpts from songs like Hendrix's "May This Be Love" and "Third Stone from the Sun," Heart's "Barracuda," Nirvana's "Smells Like Teen Spirit," and numerous others—and it was heard by many thousands of visitors at the fountain all through that summer of 2000.

Another interesting development was the ramped-up effort to produce items that could be marketed by EMP to the expected crowds. It was this imperative that finally allowed me to accomplish a long-held dream: to create a definitive compilation album of Northwest rock recordings.

While I'd helped produce other compilations in the past, they were still all limited by such practical considerations as money. That is, even when a record company like Rhino committed to issuing something like our 1987 LP, *Nuggets Volume 8: The Northwest*, the project was hemmed in by the production costs required to license the variety of songs we'd selected. An even greater impediment to accomplishing the ultimate—that is, accessing the very best recordings regardless of which corporations legally controlled them—was the seemingly insurmountable challenge of getting record companies to cooperate. To achieve this goal I needed them to set aside their habitually competitive stances and allow one (or more) of the songs they owned to be mingled with others from disparate sources.

This pipe-dream scenario hadn't ever happened, and most of us fans who'd ever hoped for it never believed it could be done. One thing's for certain: in order to pull it off, someone would need serious greenbacks to pay for legal assistance.

Asked by EMP to suggest a product-development project, I proposed that we produce the ultimate compilation of music from the first four decades of local rock. This wouldn't be a regional "greatest hits" disc—that would have meant including everything from the Fleetwoods' wispy pop doo-wop classics to headbanging heavy metal by Queensrÿche, which would have resulted in a disc that nobody (except me) would have wanted to hear. Instead, I figured, let's narrow the field down just a bit and stick to songs that totally *rock*.

Given the go-ahead, and after months of work and coordination with entertainment-law attorneys, we eventually had in hand a two-disc set I titled *Wild & Wooly: The Northwest Rock Collection*. It included a booklet with band photos and my liner notes along with tracks by forty-seven bands, licensed from about thirty-six different record companies. For the first (and probably the last) time ever, tracks by first-generation rock bands (like the Wailers, the Kingsmen, the Ventures, the Sonics, and the Dynamics) all appeared on one album together with their progeny (including Heart, Queensrÿche, Soundgarden, Nirvana, Mudhoney, the Screaming Trees, Pearl Jam, Sleater-Kinney, Built to Spill, and Modest Mouse).

I'd like to think that some of the more reticent record labels broke down and cooperated because of the obvious merit of the project, but no. It probably was the licensing fees that brought them onboard. As for the bands I'd wanted, we were very lucky there, too. We got cooperation from every band (*and* their management, *and* label) on my original wish list—well, all except for one of my absolute favorites, Alice in Chains (whose label refused), and an exciting newer group, Bikini Kill (who declined to participate, saying they didn't want to associate with a big corporate project). All in all, though, having worked on numerous LP and CD projects before and since, I can honestly say that *Wild & Wooly* is my proudest achievement and a "product" that perfectly complemented the content of the Northwest Passage gallery.

The other memorable project I was involved with during the months leading up to the grand opening was helping shape a couple of the many concerts that were being scheduled. A wide variety of major national acts were being booked in almost every venue on the entire Seattle Center campus, from Memorial Stadium to the Bagley Wright Theatre, the Flag Plaza to Key Arena. The whole thing was shaping up to be a huge music festival, a big-league event that VH1 and MTV were both contracted to broadcast live around the world. This thing was getting serious.

When asked what type of shows I'd like to see, the answer was easy: a series of concerts that would complement the Northwest Passage gallery, concerts that would showcase *both* the best-available current bands and also as many of the first-generation Northwest bands as we could persuade to reunite. Luckily, among the professionals assigned to line up bands for these various concerts was EMP's multimedia director, Jon Kertzer, and he embraced these concepts and ran with them.

After seven and a half years of preparation and planning, all that work was about to be judged both by local media (who had long expressed annoyance at our secrecy) and by legions of national and international media who'd flown to Seattle to critique this oddball museum. In the weeks leading up to the big day, I gave more than a hundred media interviews, including with the *New York Times, Newsweek, Time, Esquire, Rolling Stone*, and several of the guitar magazines. Local and regional print media included the Seattle, Bellevue, and Tacoma dailies as well as the *Seattle Weekly* and *The Rocket*. There were also interviews with specific radio and TV shows and the networks, with numerous European media outlets, and with several Web sites.

The grand opening–week itinerary commenced on the evening of June 20, and Kate and I attended a big EMP staff party that also included members of the music community who'd helped out with

---

A KISS mannequin attired in Gene Simmons's 1996 Alive Worldwide Reunion Tour "Demon" stage costume.

the new museum. What a fine time we all had finally seeing the place in operational mode! Some rockin' bands performed in EMP's great room, the Sky Church, and we all partied into the night. That whole week leading up to the opening was crammed with exciting events like this, but then June 23 arrived, bringing with it the Experience Music Project's long-awaited official grand opening.

My assignment schedule was absolutely packed with media interviews, VIP tours, and only God remembers what all else. It seemed a blur at the time, but what remains clear in my memories is watching that sunny day begin with a ceremony out front with speeches by the mayor, a county executive, Frank Gehry, Jody, and Paul. And then, before the huge crowd Paul, ceremoniously raised overhead a green glass Stratocaster-style guitar (which had been made especially for the momentous occasion by Northwest art-glass master Dale Chihuly), and with the words "Let the experience begin," smashed it to smithereens on the ground.

To the approving roar of the masses, EMP's front doors flew open, and on that first day a long queue of the first eight thousand museum members entered the $240 million, 140,000-square-foot museum to behold all the team's hard work—and a selected batch of 1,200 of our 100,000 artifacts now displayed before the eyes of the world. Having steeled myself for the worst-case scenario, I can't even begin to describe my enormous gratification that the vast majority of media critics—and an incredible number of other visitors—expressed a genuine appreciation for our efforts.

During those first three days, the museum's celebrants were entertained by a bevy of musical acts. The whole affair was organized to offer something for just about everybody. Among the sixty acts that played were James Brown, the Red Hot Chili Peppers, No Doubt, Alanis Morissette, Metallica, Dr. Dre, Snoop Dogg, Kid Rock, Filter, Joe Jackson, Rickie Lee Jones, the Eurythmics, Beck, and Matchbox Twenty. There were also free shows by Bo Diddley, Big Jay McNeely, Patti Smith, Junior Brown, Taj Mahal, and the Cold Crush Brothers.

Meanwhile, EMP's all-day Northwest Legends concert at the Mural Amphitheater attracted what was estimated to be a record-setting crowd of as many as ten thousand fans to that venue—fans who sensed that this show might be the last chance for such a major rock reunion. There on one stage we saw MC Pat O'Day providing warm introductions for the cream of the region's pioneering generation of rock 'n' rollers, including the Wailers (with original singer Gail Harris), the Dynamics (with their original guitarist Larry Coryell and singer Jimmy Hanna), Merrilee Rush, Little Bill, the Kingsmen, Paul Revere and the Raiders, and topping things off, the Ventures. Simultaneously, over at Memorial Stadium, EMP also booked a number of hot local bands, including the Screaming Trees, Built to Spill, the Fastbacks, Sir Mix-A-Lot with the Presidents, Queensrÿche, a one-off heavy metal all-star group called Scrap Metal (with members of Heart, Metal Church, Rail, and TKO), and a special Sonics "tribute group" called the New Strychnines, which was comprised of members of various bands like Mudhoney, the Young Fresh Fellows, and Girl Trouble.

All in all, it was a celebration that thrilled the city, drew throngs of attendees, and was described by *Experience Hendrix* magazine as "the biggest music party on the face of the earth." And with that, the Northwest's rock 'n' roll community witnessed the biggest and best reunion show ever mounted—and likely the best one that ever will be.

More exhilarating than these performances were the reviews that poured in after the opening. In terms of my project galleries, I was enormously pleased and flattered by the good press. The Hendrix Gallery received universal acclaim—the *Dallas Morning News* flatly deemed it "the most riveting" of all our exhibits. But the appraisals that meant the most to me were the words of thanks that both Noel Redding and Al Hendrix offered during their gallery tour.

That same review in the *Dallas Morning News* noted Quest for Volume as being "fresh and engaging" and EMP's "most scholarly exhibit." Meanwhile, the *New York Times* described it as a "thoughtful and informed exploration." The *Santa Barbara Independent* said that it "nicely chronicles the meteoric development of the electric guitar in the 20th century, with plenty of vintage models to drool over."

It was my beloved Northwest Passage—the exhibit that, besides the Hendrix Gallery, seemed to be consistently attracting the most visitors—that really drew the kudos. Our local media loved it, with the *Seattle P-I* stating that "one of the most honorable elements of EMP is the organization's efforts to peel away the commercial layers of popular music and go to its essence, its heart and soul, with stops and side trips along the way back to the music's home in African American culture. That's evident in the Northwest Passage."

The national media were also impressed with the way I'd organized our quaint little provincial story into something outsiders could enjoy. A writer for the *Washington Post* said, "A good museum makes you think, and the EMP, in its respectful, big-brained treatment of rock, is nothing if not provocative. What does it mean, historically speaking, to display one of Heart's fringed green-and-yellow costumes with the formal grandeur of an Elizabethan gown? What does a Pearl Jam PerfectScents air freshener say about pop culture? I happily mulled such thoughts as I strolled EMP's trio of galleries . . . My favorite: the quirky Northwest Passage gallery. It begins with Native American chanting and winds its way toward the growling grunge sound that put Flannel Seattle on the map . . . [F]or rock devotees who want to immerse themselves in pop-music culture and are willing to give EMP the time it deserves, this place is the real deal—raw and raucous and smart."

Rolling Stone also approved: "Northwest Passage is an illuminating example of EMP's singular approach to historical depth. The museum has no major Beatles or Rolling Stones pieces. But Northwest Passage runs the gamut from the Fender guitar used on the Kingsmen's 'Louie Louie' to Sir Mix-A-Lot's mack-daddy Stetson hat and Soundgarden's 1986 Chevy tour van."

Finally, none other than Greil Marcus, one of America's premier critics/authors, wrote in *Interview* magazine, "One of the best museum shows I ever saw was at the Centre Pompidou in Paris in 1988 . . . it was like rummaging through the attic of a whole country . . . the best story . . . It's here that the Pacific Northwest . . . stakes its claim as the true home of rock and roll."

The museum was a critical success. But beyond the critics, I was thrilled to hear that a number of musicians featured in the museum were proud of the way we'd represented them. For example, Nirvana's bassist, Krist Novoselic, shared his initial thoughts about the whole place with *Rolling Stone*: "My concern was, 'Is this gonna be a rock theme park?' [and] . . . I went away thinking, 'This is more like a university.' You could go, get some cotton candy and say, 'Let's check out Hendrix's ax.' But you can also go there on a mission, to be informed. EMP is treating rock like an art form. Making sure it is part of the permanent record." And the *New York Times* quoted him further: "I really appreciate this a lot. It's comprehensive."

Letters, e-mails, and phone calls of appreciation poured in for weeks, but of them all, the most memorable came the morning after, when Pat O'Day, being the gracious man that he always is, sent over this kind note: "I am sure you must have been overjoyed with the impact the new EMP made this last weekend. You have done so much over the years to keep the spirit of our '50s and '60s music explosion alive that this was, in a way, a tribute to you. I know it was a gratifying experience for me. Thank You!"

Although O'Day's accolades were definitely a bit over the top—what do you expect from a congenitally exuberant veteran Top-40 AM radio DJ?—and the success of EMP's grand-opening gala was clearly the result of a huge team of talented people, his nod to my dedication to raising the profile of our regional music over the decades was deeply appreciated.

FOLLOWING MY MUSE

In the weeks and months following the grand opening, I happily conducted lectures on various topics in EMP's auditorium and led gallery tours with groups of public school teachers as well as countless groups of the museum's new members. I also accompanied many VIPs, spending a memorable day with the Princeton professor Dr. Cornel West; another with the discoverer of the DNA molecule, Dr. James D. Watson; and another with the heads of the Motown Museum. Because the whole EMP building and its various exhibits had these visitors simply agog—and curious to learn more than even the exhibit labels and the MEG audio could offer—this new assignment was very rewarding.

In the midst of all this, I was still at heart a collector. In fact, even in the middle of that grand-opening weekend frenzy, I had taken time to do what I do best: acquire artifacts for EMP's collections.

That was how I found myself tearing away from one or another of those concerts to successfully bid by cell phone on some killer material from a major auction of items related to the heavy metal band KISS. At auction's end I'd nabbed a couple guitars, some handwritten lyrics, and best of all, a complete set of four stage costumes replete with mannequins designed to look just like the band members. My thought at the time was that this stuff was just so perfectly over the top, and instantly recognizable to KISS fans, that it would one day serve as the anchor for either an exhibit about that band or, thinking in broader terms, maybe even some kind of heavy metal exhibit.

Little did I expect then that I would not be at EMP long enough to help create such a show. But as 2000 slipped into 2001, nagging thoughts began to gnaw on me: I had for nearly eight years been involved in what was likely the once-in-a-lifetime experience of being able to contribute my best thinking, and all my energies, to the founding of a major new arts institution in my own hometown. I had learned more than I'd ever thought possible from some of the finest museum professionals in the world. I'd met and talked with many of music's finest players. I'd traveled widely and seen and handled some very cool things. I'd made friends and connections ranging around the planet. I'd been able to lead the development of perhaps the richest archive of rock 'n' roll artifacts on earth. I'd helped create what we all hope will be a lasting tribute to Jimi Hendrix.

And to bring things full circle, I believe that I also accomplished my own original goal of helping to salvage my hometown's music history, which a couple decades ago seemed to be slipping away largely unheralded. I think it's safe to say that partially through my long, dedicated, independent, and ongoing efforts, probably no other region of America has had its music history so systematically documented as that of the Pacific Northwest. Through the archiving of historical objects, the researching of documentary materials, the production of oral-history interviews, the publishing of many historical essays, and the mounting of public exhibits, scores of Northwest musicians and music-industry figures are now more widely known and appreciated than they were back when I first began collecting.

As a collector who'd been active for more than three decades, I'd certainly reached a career pinnacle of sorts. But now . . . I had another desire: to step aside and, well, collect my thoughts; to relax a bit, and to follow my muse wherever it led . . .

In mid-2001, as EMP's one-year anniversary approached, I made a difficult decision and gave my formal notice. In subsequent weeks, an orderly parting was arranged, and I said my farewells to Paul, Jody, and other friends at EMP, leaving them all in good spirits. Jody wrote me a note wishing me good luck and offering thanks for "all the many contributions that you have made over the last eight years." She also added, "I also hope that at least some of your writing will be about the music scene and that you will view and use EMP as the great resource that you helped create."

In announcing my departure to the staff, Chris Bruce wrote that "Pete has given so much to EMP. The collection will live as a lasting legacy. In particular, EMP's commitment to the Northwest is a testament to Pete's own commitment and passion about the creativity that has existed in his beloved Northwest. He has been one of the very few individuals who has been involved in EMP from that mythical 'day one,' and who has had so much to do with what it is today. As such, he leaves with a great deal of pride in a job well done, and a great foundation for those who follow." Reading that, I gulped. As kind as the testimony was, I suddenly felt like I was reading my own obituary.

Word began spreading that I'd made the big move, and a few notices appeared in the papers, including one in the *Seattle Weekly* that inquired, "What's up with Peter Blecha leaving his post as senior curator at Experience Music Project? It's a big loss for the museum, which benefited from his unparalleled knowledge of Northwest music history."

Perhaps so, but it was I who had benefited from the unbelievable opportunities and experiences I'd had in my eight and a half years with the museum project. In the end, I guess I just realized that it was the initial creative phase—the front-end process of helping to conceptualize the museum and some of its exhibits—rather than the operational day-to-day phase of helping run an actual institution that had most interested me. Now, that too had its rewarding moments, but I was just itching to get back in touch with my own creative muse and to spend some time writing books, writing songs, and maybe just doing some personal collecting, but at a more casual pace.

EPILOGUE

Well, so much for the notion of lazing about and languidly doing nothing for a while in order to decompress after the maniacal pace of the EMP years: within days of moving on from the museum (which has enjoyed nearly three million visitors to date), I was immersed in various new endeavors. Among them was beginning the writing of *Taboo Tunes*, a book on the history of music censorship. In addition, I began serving as contributing editor (of music and pop culture) for the online regional-history Web site HistoryLink.org—a great forum for writing about various aspects of local history. Before long, I also accepted an invitation to serve on the advisory committee for the long-planned Northwest African American Museum (NAAM), a promising project that continues to make progress toward its ambitious goals.

Because I have provided historical consultation to producers at various media firms, record labels, and radio stations over the years, I decided to formalize that situation. I launched a freelance business called Muse Consulting Services. My first client turned out to be a most interesting one.

I received a call one day from Seattle's veteran record producer Jerry Dennon, whose biggest claim to fame was that of being the fellow behind the success of the Kingsmen's "Louie Louie." He wondered if I would be willing to help him market the gold record he'd received upon the one millionth sale of that disc back in 1965. The task sounded like fun, so in December 2003 I took it on and came up with a plan to sell it on eBay. Using what I had learned in generating publicity from my days at EMP, we started with a press release about the sale, which sparked headlines across the country and included coverage by CNN, CBS News, and ABC News. With all the attendant hoopla, about fifteen hundred curious folks visited the auction site to watch the bidding action, a good number participated, and in the end, the record drew a nice high bid of $7,700.

The *Taboo Tunes* book project also turned into a great excuse to stage another exhibit. On May 7, 2004, the book launched with a party at a local art gallery. At the new exhibit, Broken Record: The Graphics of Censorship, I was thrilled that friends Krist Novoselic and Mark Arm both served as guest DJs spinning "taboo tunes." In all, nearly four hundred beer-drinking and wine-sipping revelers attended, and much fun was had when the crowd was handed about three hundred scratchy 78 (and worthless) records to shatter all over the floor.

It's important to note, by the way, that Broken Record was probably possible to curate *only* because of the existence of eBay—my source for many of the items eventually placed on display. There simply would have been no other way to locate so many rare artifacts in such a limited, couple-year time frame.

That is something I can confidently state even as a relative eBay newbie. You see, I'd been monitoring the auction site occasionally for a number of years—using it mainly as a way to research comparable prices for various artifacts that were offered to me while at EMP. But until I'd departed the museum I'd never bid in any of their auctions. Then I sold that "Louie Louie" gold record, and soon I found myself becoming inexorably drawn into the process. I didn't really *want* this new source for acquiring stuff. I had no real desire to start up any new collections, and I haven't really. But, as measured by the more than five hundred different eBay transactions I've engaged in thus far, I have not been entirely successful in curbing my interest in cool Northwest artifacts. While I consciously realize that it is not my duty to carry on with archiving historical music artifacts from this region—after all, there is a museum in town that does that now—it seems that I just can't shake off a decades-old habit of nabbing interesting items I run across while out junking around. Having studied local music history for so long, I simply cannot resist a truly rare find. I mean, what else should I do when some elusive item finally shows up after I'd been keeping an eye out for it all these years?

So, no, I haven't started up any new collections. Instead, the basement in Kate's and my home has been seeing the steady accumulation of old records and rock posters—recent collecting finds that, I guess, technically represent "phase two" of my old, original love for Northwest music. Mine is an irrepressible collecting commitment that I now see will probably end only on the hopefully distant day when I pull up to the happy hunting grounds of that great flea market in the sky.

.

INDEX TO PHOTOGRAPHY

ABOUT THE AUTHOR

Peter Blecha, a music historian and pop-culture critic, was the former senior curator at Experience Music Project (EMP), an eight-year post he held since the start of the museum's planning to a year after its doors opened. Prior to working at EMP, Blecha had been a radio DJ, a columnist for the Seattle music magazine *The Rocket*, and the founder/curator of the Northwest Music Archive. The latter project, and its subsequent collection of more than 20,000 artifacts, led him to be considered since the 1980s as the preeminent Northwest music historian.

Blecha has served as a board member with JAMPAC (Joint Artists & Music Promotions Political Action Committee). His writings about early electric guitar technology led him to an advisory post as a member of the Indiana University–associated Center for Research into the Anthropological Foundations of Technology (CRAFT). He also serves on the advisory committee for Seattle's Northwest African American Museum (NAAM).

Blecha is the author of the book *Taboo Tunes* (Backbeat, 2004) as well as the essay "Wired Wood: The Origins of the Electric Guitar" (1996). His writings have also appeared in such periodicals as *Life* magazine, *Vintage Guitar*, *DISCoveries*, *Seattle Weekly*, *Radio Guide*, *Feedback*, *The Monthly*, www.HistoryLink.org, and the liner notes on numerous LPs and CDs. He lives in Seattle with his wife, Kate.